The Innkeeper of Jericho
and Other Eye-Witnesses from the Beginning

Philip Liebelt

Published by Immortalise via Ingram Spark

© Philip Liebelt 2021

All rights reserved. This book or any portion thereof may not be reproduced or used in any manner whatsoever without the express written permission of the author, except for the use of brief quotations in a book review.

First Printing, 2021

ISBN print: 978-0-6488957-5-6
ebook: 978-0-6488957-6-3

Typesetting and cover layout by Ben Morton
Cover images by Dustin and Philip Liebelt

The Innkeeper of Jericho

and Other Eye-Witnesses from the Beginning

Philip Liebelt

Also by Philip Liebelt:

Making Connections: Jesus Stories and Ours; Telling and Hearing Parables in Luke, JBCE, Melbourne, 1996.

Gentle Rain on Parched Earth: Worship Resources for Rural Settings, (Ed.) with Noel Nicholls JBCE, Melbourne, 1996 & Morehouse Pub. Co., New York, 1997.

Carrying Rainbows of Hope: Liturgical Resources for use after Disasters and Personal Tragedies, (Edited) National Disaster Fund Trust Committee of the Uniting Church in Australia Assembly, Sydney, 2003

YouTube: Philip Liebelt
Storytelling channel where some of these stories are told.

Table of Contents

Introduction 1
The Innkeeper of Jericho 7
Zacchaeus – The Back Story 15
Jairus – A Leader of the Synagogue 25
The Temptations of Jesus According to a Former Apprentice Devil 29
A Blind Man sees Jesus enter Jerusalem 35
Demos – former Jailer of Philippi 43
Philip's Nephew's Lunch 51
Nicodemus – A Member of the Sanhedrin on the first Easter Day 57
Rich, Black, Outcast, 'Half-Man' 63
The Writer of Mark Contemplating the Writing of a Gospel 67
A Nazarene Jew who found a New Faith 75
Joel of Capernaum 85
Grace at a Pharisee's Table 91
"How Strong is your faith?" 101
An Israeli Shepherd speaks 107
The Road to Jerusalem 113
Bibliography 125

Introduction

Since 1990 I have been telling Biblical stories in the style of the Network of Biblical Storytellers. That means telling them 'by heart', having internalised them rather than just memorising, as the latter can become a purely rote learning exercise. Here is not the place to go into details of that process. However, the preparation of stories for telling does involve the teller looking at some of the background and cultural context of the stories. This cannot always be conveyed in the telling, if one is to stay with the text, though it shapes that telling.

I had already been writing first-person or eye-witness stories, and this background to Biblical stories became a new source of material. This has continued spasmodically through to assembling this collection; so it represents thirty years of writing. Many people have gone before me with their own similar types of stories, so there is nothing unique or original in the concept.

Then in 1998 I also began telling a ninety-minute collection of stories from Luke's Gospel, probably less than a third of this long gospel. In the opening verses the writer suggests the sources used in this compilation of stories of the life and ministry of Jesus.

Since many have undertaken to set down an orderly account of the events
that have been fulfilled among us, just as they were handed on to us by those
who from the beginning were eye-witnesses and servants of the word,
I too decided, after investigating everything carefully from the very first,
to write an orderly account for you, most excellent Theophilus,
so that you may know the truth concerning the things
about which you have been instructed. (Luke 1:1-4)

It is easy to believe that those who witnessed Jesus' life and ministry would have shared their experiences with later converts who followed the teachings of Jesus, and were the forerunners of the 'Christian' Church. Clearly there was a gap between these events and when scholars believe they were written down as 'gospels'. So these stories had an oral form before they were written down. Even after they were written down, most people still relied on hearing the stories told (or read) because there was no ability to mass print manuscripts and because literacy levels were low.

There are stories in the gospels when only one person plus Jesus or someone like an angel, was present. Take for example the annunciation stories of Mary and Zechariah in Luke 1. Clearly, those individuals were the first eye-witnesses to pass on such stories.

This then is the thinking behind my collection of first-person stories. Not that the above comments mean they are all from Luke, although even when other sources are used Lucan references are an additional influence. I also draw on Luke's second book, 'Acts'. All involve a certain amount of creative thinking or licence. Often these are stories of characters not central to the gospel story or who are just presumed to have been there somewhere in the background, or mentioned in passing in the text. For example, the lead story of 'The Innkeeper of Jericho' is told by one who gets only a fleeting reference in the parable of the Good Samaritan.

When I engage in Biblical storytelling, as described above, I tell the text as it is, without significantly rewriting it. Some hearers have commented that Biblical Storytellers take a literal view of the scriptures. I would prefer to say that I am taking a neutral view of them (to the extent that this can be done), or that in that situation I am not setting out to give a particular interpretation of them. In the telling, I am not wishing to engage in a conversation about whether the scriptures should be viewed through literal or 'fundamentalist' eyes or more 'liberal' ones. I hope I am presenting them so as to still allow listeners to take whatever theological stance they feel comfortable with. Of course any telling is still an 'interpretation' at some level, by virtue of the way it is told and the inferences or body language that are used. Tellings of the same story by different people will not be the same; and nor will tellings on different occasions by the same teller.

The same applies to these stories. When approaching the scriptures to write a first- person story I am not wishing to enter into a discussion about whether this actually happened the way it has been recorded. Again, I am at some level putting an interpretation on a story. Indeed, if I am introducing some fictional background information, such interpretation is inevitable. I just don't want the distraction of how 'literal' or how 'liberal' that interpretation is, to get in the way of people hearing the story.

In this story writing process I often use a technique called "stitching stories together" which Richard Jensen introduced as a style of narrative preaching. It is part of a process of "thinking in stories" rather than the traditional preaching style of "thinking in ideas". My added spin to this is to put it into first-person which he was not automatically suggesting. I was fortunate enough to attend a weeklong workshop with Richard at Berkley, California, in 1994, although in hindsight I was probably already writing in that style before then. He wrote about it in his book "Thinking in Story: preaching in a post-literate age".[1]

"Stitching stories together" involves telling on one occasion different stories from different places in the scriptures that have a common theme or are

---

1 Richard A. Jensen, "Thinking in Story: Preaching in a Post-Literate Age", C.S.S. Publishing Co., Lima, Ohio, 1993

linked through a character. In a sermon, that might simply mean telling a number of such stories linked to a Lectionary reading, with little commentary or sermonising in between or doing this in the introduction and conclusion. I share Richard's keenness to see this commentary kept to a minimum so as to allow the stories to stand on their own. In my case it is about weaving these stories together into one person's story, where the "commentary" becomes that person filling in some gaps that the scriptures don't address. A simple example of this might be one person's recollection of the stories leading up to and including Jesus' death and resurrection.

Another example is my "Grace at a Pharisee's Table", when I speculate that one woman in one gospel story may have been the same person as appears in another story in another gospel. This is also the only time in my eye-witness stories that I have told in a woman's voice. This story, included here, was one of the more recently written ones. I have previously not presumed to be able to think or tell a story as a woman would. This story also takes a more poetic form than other stories, for that seemed to be how it needed to be told. (Incidentally, I have not told or read it publicly, but always ask a woman to do so, particularly as it is a first-person account.)

It will already be evident that what I am doing in these stories involves some creative thinking. This includes imagining the tellers of the story being in some mysterious existence in a floating time period. In some cases they are familiar with other stories from their earthly time or other times. Often they converse with the audience as if they have come from heaven, and are familiar with modern-day expressions, or even predict them. This 'playing around' is not to be taken too seriously. It also creates a question of where to end the story; for presumably characters caught up in eternity know the end of the story, not just that part of it in which they originally appeared.

Another aspect of this is that my stories often cross between gospels. There are certain stories unique to only one gospel, but which have connections with stories in other gospels. Sometimes I choose to ignore these connections and other times I bring together those stories from different gospels, as in "Grace at a Pharisee's table" (referred to above). If, for example, we consider the resurrection stories we know that different eye-witnesses clearly have different recollections of the events following Jesus' rising. There are also mysteries left for us to ponder. Examples of this are the ending of Mark's Gospel, and the questions Luke 24:12 (omitted from some versions), 24:24 and 24:34 raise, when set next to the broader story. Such questions are fertile ground for the creative mind. But it should also be noted that these stories are not trying to do a theological analysis of the gospel stories or answer all the questions they raise.

A comment ought also be made about the layout I usually use with these stories. Growing out of my preparation in learning Biblical Stories for telling, is the need to structure them for ease of reading, learning and telling. It is harder to work with text that is right-hand and left-hand justified as this Introduction is and as the text of modern day Bibles usually is. If this were not so, the Bibles would be considerably thicker. We naturally pause (ever so briefly) at the end of a line of text, whether or not there is a hard pause created by punctuation or the end of a clause or phrase. Where text is justified, such a line might end with a broken-word hyphen, or a word like "the" or "a" which is not where one would want to pause. So Biblical Storytellers reposition the text so natural pauses are at the end of the line. This aids the flow of the story. So what I have just written would appear like this:

Where text is justified,
it means a line might end with a broken-word hyphen,
or a word like "the" or "a", which is not where one would want to pause.
So Biblical Storytellers reposition the text
                      so that natural pauses are at the end of the line.
This aids the flow of the story.

Accordingly, I have laid most stories out, to make them easier to read (aloud), learn and tell. I encourage those reading in Church or any public setting to do the same, if the text that is being read is justified.

In order to keep this as a collection of stories, rather than a commentary on stories from scriptures, I have not provided exhaustive references of where I have found the background information. The reader is invited to accept that the research has been done, or might be encouraged to do their own work to learn more about the mainly cultural information that has informed these stories. One of the major influences on my writing, storytelling and preaching is the late Rev. Dr. Kenneth E. Bailey who "spent forty years living and teaching New Testament in Egypt, Lebanon, Jerusalem and Cyprus, and has written many books in English and Arabic."[2]

I also offer this collection at a time that I am writing a book on Luke's Gospel, influenced by the telling of it mentioned above. That book aims to help people to see the bigger picture of the stories, than we usually get from a piecemeal hearing or reading of them. Hopefully both of these works will help readers recognise the oral form the gospels had before they were written down.

---

2   Dustcover of Kenneth E. Bailey, *"Jesus through Middle Eastern Eyes: Cultural Studies in the Gospels"*, IVP Academic, Illinois, 2008

Introduction

Finally, I want to acknowledge that most of these stories have been told or read to audiences, or congregations where introduced in worship. Feedback has led to changes. I like to think of them as "living" scripts. Therefore I appreciate the support and encouragement I have received in the Uniting Churches in Australia that I have served in during my ordained ministry: South Woden (in Canberra), East Keilor-Airport West, Balwyn, Elsternwick and in the regions of the South West (then Presbytery of Mitchell) and Gippsland (all in Victoria). And as always I thank my wife, Helen, and sons, Dustin and Ty, for their patient support as I have embarked on a story journey that has taken me across the world.

Philip Liebelt, June 2020

The Innkeeper of Jericho
(Luke 10:25 -37)

It is interesting work running an inn!
I know from first-hand experience
      because I have been running the Jericho inn for 20 years now.
Used to run the inn at Bethlehem; but that's another story for another time.
You meet all sorts of people, and boy! I could tell you a story or two.
In fact if you stick around, I will.

But I'm giving it all up now.
Packing up and moving on; although I don't know what to yet.
I'm sure it will be exciting though.
In fact the whole reason I am doing it is exciting!
Before I get to that though, let me tell you the whole story.
You see, what's happening now, really all started some time back.

It was a quietish part of the afternoon on what had been a fairly uneventful day.
Usually someone comes in with a tale of travels;
      or there's a character that's just interesting to meet.
This day there had been no one!

Well, a priest came in – white as a ghost, he was!
And panting as though he had run the last bit of his journey –
      even though he was on a donkey;
            I had noted with one eye on the courtyard.
I gave him a drink. He flopped down in a heap.
After he had settled, he told me what had happened.
He was travelling the fourteen miles home from Jerusalem
      after doing his stint in the Temple.
Let me just digress a moment and tell you about that road;
      it is a dire trip for anyone, with desolate sections through the desert.
The winding road sometimes passes through narrow gaps
      between high rugged cliffs,
            when you cannot see far in front of you, because of blind corners.
All the while, you are travelling down,
      for Jericho is some 3300 feet lower than Jerusalem.
It has excellent hiding places for thugs and robbers!

So, a distance ahead of the priest, he saw a lone traveller; a young man, on foot.

Every so often, he would disappear,
        as he went around a corner midst the rocky cliffs.
Suddenly, within earshot, but out of sight,
        the young man was set upon by thieves,
                who beat him up,
                stripped him
                and left him lying on the roadside.
The priest heard him crying out as all this unfolded.

He had not known what to do. In fact, he feared for his own life.
He thought the first thing he ought to do was to hide for a while,
        hoping he was far enough back not to have been seen by the robbers.
So he tried to hide his donkey behind a rock and keep it quiet.
No easy thing, I'm sure.
He stayed there for what seemed an eternity,
        hoping they wouldn't turn back his way.
They didn't!

Even when he thought the coast was clear he was wary.
Were there another road home, he would have taken it.
As he came to the bend in the road, where he knew the victim lay,
        his heart beat faster and he goaded his beast.
When the fellow came into view,
        the priest could see he was badly cut and bruised;
                covered in blood, dust and flies; his clothes in tatters.
He lay quite still but groaning a little.
Since his clothes were badly ripped, and knowing the man could not speak,
the priest had no way of knowing to what caste or race the man belonged.
He manoeuvred his beast to ensure
        he stayed the required distance from a bleeding,
                and possibly dead man… (*pause*)…to avoid becoming unclean.
And then he hastened past!

"I would normally have stopped and helped a needy traveller –
        depending on his type;
                have no doubt about that."
The priest spoke with some urgency.
"But I feared the thieves would return.
And I couldn't risk becoming unclean before I returned to the Temple, could I?"
He appealed to me for assurance.
"But I said a speedy prayer to Yahweh, as I hurried past.

He is my witness that I did!
You understand, I had no choice!"
He continued to plead for my support.

He'd calmed down by the time he left me.
Either getting his story out had helped, or the wine had worked its usual magic.
As he went, I assured him that if anyone called in, going the other way,
I'd ask him to keep an eye out for the victim – and warn them of the robbers.
I pondered the priest's response to his dilemma.
I wondered if his failure to help the young man was justified or even justifiable.
I had to ask myself, "What would I have done?"

I hadn't worked through all these questions fully
      when a second traveller arrived.
Talkative, aggressive and assured, he was – unlike the priest!
He strutted in and talked of his journey – at first in a general sort of way -
      but then he got increasingly animated.

"Hardly safe to travel on these roads anymore!" He complained.
"Rocks are full of thieves and bullies!
Why can't the Romans patrol the routes between major towns?
Decent citizens should feel safe going about their business. Not terrified!
It's like your freedom has been taken away.

"Why even just now, I passed by a fellow, beaten and left for dead!
His blood was drying and flies crawled on his shroud of dust.
Dreadful sight he was!

"Saw a priest on a donkey, turn a bend ahead of me.
He may have seen the attack happen.
But he certainly passed by and left the man there.
Well, I didn't have a beast!"
He added quickly as if my body language displayed scepticism.
"What could I do for him? If a priest can't help, why should I?
I mean, I'm a Levite, right?
And I know they think our role in the Temple isn't as important as theirs.
But we still have more important things to be doing
      than tending the careless and unfortunate
           who fall victim to such treacherous stretches of road.
I mean, we have to keep ourselves clean, too, for our Temple duties, you know!
Citizens would be rightly worried if they knew we were out

picking up dead and bleeding bodies off the roadways.
People who could even be foreigners!
And then, of course, going off to the Temple to perform sacrifices!
We'd be shamed! Unclean for life we could be!
We've got a job to do!"

He returned to his former theme.
It seemed there was a duty here for everyone but him.
"If army patrols didn't deter gangs doing this sort of thing,
    at least they could ensure the victims got proper care.
It's not up to the likes of you or me to be doing anything. Is it?"
But he pressed on, not really allowing me to answer that question.
"When I got into town, I passed the information on, of course.
Bet the priest didn't bother. Did you see that priest?"
(He gave me no time to respond in any way.)
"Do you think he would have done anything?
I expect it was too late by the time I got here. Probably, dead by then!"

When he paused to draw breath, long enough for me to get a word in,
I was ready to engage him in vigorous debate
    and question his callous and uncaring attitude.
I was incensed with him, more than with the priest
 who nearer to the action, was scared and didn't or couldn't think straight.
I say, I was about to challenge him; I didn't get the chance.
Two things happened to prevent me following through on this.
Possibly the bit I did get out alerted the Levite,
    for he suddenly "needed to be on his way!"
Even so, my growing anger was such that I might have blocked his way,
    so that I could have my say.
However, him getting up to leave, coincided with a commotion outside.
So as the Levite went to the front door,
    I was obliged to go to the court yard,
        to see what was happening out there.
As I opened the door, I was greeted by a large, affable man.
His warmth shone in his face; but could also be felt in his very presence.
Just as instantly my reaction to his demeanour
    was swallowed by distrust and discomfort.
He was a Samaritan! Scum of the earth!
Like most Jews I had little time for any of them.
I wouldn't serve them in my inn if I could be choosy about my customers.
Not after what they have done to my people over the years!

The Innkeeper of Jericho

"What do you want?" I asked – gruffly, I guess!
My last guest, and now this one, left me in no mood for pleasantries.
"A room!" He replied pleasantly, choosing not to read me.
    "Have you got one to spare?"
"Not for your kind!" I retorted.
"It isn't just for me," he persisted.
"I have found this poor unfortunate man on the side of the road,
    having been set upon and left for dead.
I have tended his wounds, but will care for him overnight
    whilst I do my business here in Jericho.
Then if you will take over, I will pay you what I have,
    and repay you any extra when I am here next."
I was floored!
Deep inside me, I rumbled with discomfort and a mixture of other emotions.
I couldn't see whether the victim was a Jew, but guessed that he was;
    but tended and cleaned by a Samaritan!
He had disarmed my rejection of his Samaritanism,
    by giving me no chance to speak of it.
So, here was one, whom I would not willingly give the time of day,
    helping this poor fellow in a way my other two customers had refused.
Whilst I was greatly more at ease with their company;
    I was incensed by their refusal to help.
Furthermore, this Samaritan pays in full for the care of a Jewish enemy,
    who clearly has no money to pay.
        Care I should willingly give freely.
Not only that; he risks the vengeance of the victim's family;
    who seeing him involved would have assumed the worst.

Well, I did care for this poor soul, and nursed him back to health;
    and the Samaritan was true to his word.
Thus his actions challenged my prejudices;
    whilst I had thought I was above those who had refused to help.
He challenged those of the patient also;
    for as I talked to him I became aware of two things.
He too was moved by the kindness of someone with whom
    he would not normally mix.
Indeed he admitted he would avoid passing through Samaria if he could.
A bit like me wanting to reject a Samaritan's patronage.

Furthermore, I was deeply moved by this victim also.
He had a depth of grace and warmth I had seldom experienced.

Perhaps I had only experienced it once before – just days ago –
> in that Samaritan, who had brought him to my inn.
His warm eyes looked into mine and seemed to pierce my soul.
I felt he could see everything that I might want to hide. Like those prejudices!
But his was a look of compassion, not of judgement;
one which haunted me until today and showed up my continued failings!

Yes, haunted me until today!
You see, there's more to this story, that happened nearly ten years ago.
Today, this event and its characters returned to me – larger than life.
I was at the market place buying supplies,
> when I came upon a rabbi talking to a large crowd.
The scenario was not uncommon; the rabbi seemed like any other.
Some of the crowd were clearly his students and disciples;
> others questioned him
>> with challenges and even aggression; as is also common.

For instance a teacher of the Law called out,
> "Teacher, what must I do to inherit eternal life?"
The question was surely a test, for how can one inherit eternal life?
But the response threw the attack back on the questioner.
"What is written in the Law?" he asked. "How do you read it?"
Although unsettled by the question, there was a smugness in the lawyer's reply,
> which was rattled off from memory,
>> for he knew his scriptures well,
>>> as you might expect of a student of the Law!
"Love the Lord your God with all your heart,
> and with all your soul,
> and with all your strength
> and with all your mind.
And your neighbour as yourself."
This response received encouragement. "So, do this and you will live!"

But the lawyer searched for more. I think he wanted to justify himself,
> for he asked: "And who is my neighbour?"
He wasn't ready for the story given in reply. Nor was I!
Although it didn't quite knock me over as it might have
> – and I'll tell you why in a moment.

The rabbi began:
"A certain man was going down from Jerusalem to Jericho

when he fell among thieves who stripped him and beat him
and left him half dead."
And sure enough he went on to talk of a priest and then a Levite
who both refused to stop and tend his wounds.
And how a Samaritan, of all people, came along,
tended his wounds and took him to an inn,
and paid the innkeeper for his care.
"That's me!" I almost shouted.

But I knew now it was time for me to leave my inn.
I must be about following this teacher
and exploring his love practically and totally in my life.
That teacher is Jesus,
who I now know to be the Messiah we Jews have long awaited.
I believe that he alone has the words of eternal life.

As soon as I saw Jesus in the marketplace, I recognised him.
A Samaritan once brought him to me – bruised, battered and bleeding –
and I grew to love him as I nursed him back to health.
The full weight of what Jesus pondered in those few days
the weight of a Samaritan's compassion even for an enemy –
took ten years to sink into me.

As a wounded man, he was saved from death
through the costly show of unexpected love by the Samaritan.
This Jesus, so often rejected as an outsider,
has cast himself in the role of that Samaritan,
and comes to bind the wounds of the suffering.
In so doing, he shows us God's unexpected and unconditional love.
I must follow Jesus to Jerusalem, on that dreadful road,
and learn more of this love;
even though I do not know what awaits us there.

---

† This story came about from two different influences.
I heard the late Clifford Warne, a great Sydney storyteller, say at a Christian Arts School in Canberra, that he told the story of the Good Samaritan through the eyes of the Innkeeper. I didn't hear him do it, but it sowed a seed in my mind that germinated some time later.

Then in John Aurelio's book *Myth Man: A Storyteller's Jesus (* Crossroad Pub. Co., New York, 1992*)* was the suggestion that Jesus created this parable from an experience he personally had.
These two ideas came together naturally.

Zacchaeus – The Back Story

(Luke 2:1; 5: 27-32; 15: 1-2; 18:9-14; 19: 1-10. Matthew 28:16; Mark 16:7; Acts 1: 15; 2: 1-4)

There are three groups of people in the world;
>Those who can count and those who cannot! *(Pause)*

Seriously, though two things are certain in life – death and taxes!
Someone greater than I, Zacchaeus, will say this one day
>and be remembered for it.

My people, the Jews, knew it to be true, though.
Indeed taxes[3] seem to have been around forever,
>and probably will be into the future.

I'm told the ancient Greeks had taxes.
The Egyptians had their grains taxed
>in preparation for the seven year famine
>and helped feed my ancestors, Joseph's brothers and family.

And taxes don't go away either!
King Solomon had a Temple tax to build that great building –
>and it lasted a thousand years.
>>The tax I mean, not the building.

Many years later we would be taxed by foreigners
>who invaded then controlled our country
>>- the Persians, the Greeks, and the god-forsaken Romans.

You may be wondering how I know so much about taxes.
Well – I pay them; and I collected them.
For years I was chief tax collector in Jericho.
So I know about taxes. And I know about death!
And I also know about something else that is just as certain.
Before I tell you what that is, let me tell you my story.
It is a story of pain and suffering, but has ended in joy and freedom.
Under the Romans we have been constantly and harshly taxed.
The Romans built great bridges, roads and canals;
>but it seems the main reason was in order to collect a toll.

---

3 Background information on taxes and tax collectors in Biblical times are taken from the entries on Tax and Tax Collector in *The Interpreters Dictionary of the Bible* Vol. 4, Abingdon Press, Nashville,1984 (14th. Printing. First Published 1962) Pp 520-522

The Innkeeper of Jericho and other Eye-Witnesses from the Beginning

Can you imagine that – charging a toll so people can use a public road!
Then our own King Herod placed a tax on the produce of the land;
    and a sales tax on all items bought and sold.
Can you imagine THAT – a tax on everything we buy and sell?
    Goods and services!
So we had a land tax – payable in kind or in money;
    road tolls;
    a tax on personal property;
    export and import customs at sea ports and city gates,
    and down in Jerusalem, they even had a house tax.
And did I mention the Temple tax?
People needed the right currency
    for their offerings at the Temple in Jerusalem;
    so there were money changers there
    charging exorbitant rates of exchange.
And only the best beasts could be sacrificed, sold at premium prices.

Over thirty years ago, the Roman Emperor – Augustus it was –
    even called a census, throughout the whole country.
We had to go back to our family's town of origin
    to be registered, so as to pay our taxes.
My family lived in Capernaum then, but we had to come back
    to be registered in Jericho, our home town.
And I ended up staying here!

So, you can imagine collecting all these taxes was a major exercise.
I guess that's where I come in!
I was a dumpy kid; not very strong. Not very tall!
I couldn't do a lot of the hard labour jobs, or be in the army,
    so I was fortunate to get an education.
Learnt languages; learnt to read and write; a privilege few had.
I was fascinated with keeping records and remembering facts.
    I was good at it!
I knew where everyone lived and could remember all the family names.
You name it; I had it all here! (*points to head*)

Well, all that education didn't do me much good!

Zacchaeus – The Back Story

I was never going to be a rabbi or a teacher.
And as I said before, I wasn't strong enough to do physical jobs.
Finally, my family gave me some money and sent me on my way.
I was determined to get rich
      and show them I could achieve something in life.
But this led to me making the biggest mistake I ever made.
Oh, that I could undo that decision and the years that followed.
You see, I used that money to bid at auction for the right to collect taxes.
My education made me ideally suited to the work.

From there I later became a chief tax collector,
      in charge of all tax collectors in Jericho.
But I was rejected by my own people
      and as hated as the Romans who employed me.
The richer I became – the poorer in spirit I was.
Tax officers are not popular anywhere,
      because no one likes paying taxes.
This is no doubt the case in free countries
      as much as in our occupied one.
But, under Roman rule,
      we tax collectors were especially despised and degraded.
My people hated the domination they were under –
      even though the Romans brought some good,
            with their bridges, roads and viaducts.
We were oppressed under military rule. Of this we were reminded
      everyday by the presence of soldiers in our streets.
            We looked forward to freedom.
Revolutionary groups conspired in secret,
      taking opportunities to make public attacks on the regime!
Some might call them acts of terrorism; but certainly acts of revolution.
Because the Romans were a pagan nation,
      those most strongly opposed to them,
            believed any act of submission
                  – like paying taxes – was an act against Yahweh!
More responsible leaders didn't go so far, but looked on the taxes
      as an imposition by a foreign conqueror,
            not fair requirement to maintain social order.

What-is-more the amounts taken in taxes were excessive,
>   making both Roman officials and tax collectors, rich.
I did not anticipate how entering into the employ of the Romans
>   would make me such an outcast of society.
I had sold myself into the service of foreign oppressors
>   against my own people,
>   >   who then identified me as being 'one of them.'
In reality I was neither Jew nor Roman.
I might just as well have been a slave.
Constant contact with foreigners also made me unclean
>   – rejected in another way!
The demands of the contract I committed to,
>   meant I had to steal by taking more than my due.
This became a vicious circle,
>   for with the support and encouragement of the Romans
>   >   it became too easy to take more and more than I should have
>   >   >   – and so I became very rich!
But money can't buy you happiness!
Further, my position was so despised that:
>   I was disqualified from other public offices;
>   I could not be a witness in court;
>   I was not allowed to attend the synagogue;
>   My work regularly required me to break the Sabbath law;
>   My family was tarnished with the same brush and rejected me.
Tax collectors were considered in the same category as murderers,
>   robbers, money changers and common sinners,
>   >   even prostitutes and adulterers
>   >   >   – none of whom were considered well
>   >   >   >   in my community and culture.
Nor could I use my money for good – it too was tainted;
for to touch the wealth of one who gains it unlawfully, shares his guilt.

And it gets worse! I could not get out!
 If I had given up the job,
>   I had no possibility of being employed elsewhere,
>   despite my education

and the experience that working with money
> and records gave me.

A murderer doesn't get too many job interviews either!
In my loneliness and remorse I sunk deeper into despair. Depression!
My life was surrounded with the finest possessions,
but I would gladly have traded it all for a happier life and some friends.

Then I heard a story that raised new hope for me.
I told you before I was originally from Capernaum.
I kept contact with a few acquaintances there
> who still acknowledged me.

Also, we tax collectors stuck together – we had to!
Afterall, we were all in the same boat; like a colony of lepers!

Well, a tax collector from Capernaum, Levi was his name,
> told me how a rabbi came to his tax booth one day
>> and called Levi to "follow him."

Immediately, he felt a sense of release.
> A way out of the predicament I also was in.

This rabbi treated Levi as a real person, not an outcast;
> valuing his presence and hospitality.

His name was Jesus and Levi became one of his students.
No, more – a disciple!
Levi spoke of him being the Messiah. This I found hard to believe.
But I hung out for the next instalments of Levi's stories,
> because he was clearly getting a love and acceptance
>> none of us were used to, and all of us desired.

For example, the day Jesus 'called' him,
> Levi invited Jesus home to a meal with some of his friends
>> and Jesus' other followers.

You understand from what I have said
> who Levi's friends would have been.

Apparently, some Pharisees caught wind of this and turned up.
Meals in our culture are open to the general community.
They were indignant that a supposedly good and religious teacher
> was mixing with such outcasts.

Levi told how Jesus used a current proverb to respond:
> "Those who are well have no need of a doctor,
>   but only those who are sick.
> I came to call not the righteous, but sinners to repentance."

In all the confusion and sadness of my life,
> this gave me a glimmer of hope,
>> if only I knew what to do with it.

Stories from Levi came too few and far between,
> as he travelled the country with this Jesus.

It was clear though that here was a man
> who did not treat us and other sinners like dirt.

He ate with them, spending quality hospitality time with them,
> even though he was roundly criticised for it.

In our culture to eat with someone
> meant you valued them and wanted to get to know them better.

This did not mean he condoned our sin – he looked for change;
> but offered help so it could be achieved.

The recognition of my sinful life and remorse
> weighed heavily on my soul.

I even took the opportunity, when in Jerusalem on business,
> to visit the Temple.

My uncleanness kept me from the altar area.
That was like modern day believers having to pray out in the foyer.
I had gone at the time for prayers and sacrifice to be put right with God.
> Atonement, we call it!

I just beat my breast and wailed to God for mercy.
I went home wondering if I could ever enjoy such a blessing from God.
I felt so completely beyond forgiveness.
In the main body of the Temple I saw and heard a Pharisee also at prayer.
> He stood apart from others,
>> seemingly concerned not to brush up against anyone.
>
> He feared contact with someone who was unclean like me.
> He kept away from us physically; but his prayer didn't!
> He spoke so loudly even I could hear him from outside.
> "I thank you, God, that I am not like others."

He listed off a number of sinful groups and gestured towards me.
He boasted that he fasted twice a week,
>   when only once was required,
and tithed of all he had
>   when the Law didn't demand such a sacrifice.
Whilst he was boastful, arrogant and judgemental,
>   I was left wondering if he might go home right with God,
>   >   when I had no hope of that.

But , my prayer was answered; though not as I had expected.
>   I have learnt since that God does this.
One day, as I travelled to visit a tax booth, I saw a large crowd.
I overheard that Jesus was coming to Jericho.
I had little time to work out a way of doing it,
>   but I just wanted to see who he was.
You will have gauged by now that I am no one's friend.
A person of my short stature had no chance of seeing over the crowd,
>   and no one was about to let me through.
>   >   Just "What's *he* doing here?" taunts.
So I did the first thing that came into my head.
>   I climbed a sycamore tree by the road.
Just so that I could get a glimpse of Jesus!
I thought such a sighting might lift my spirits –
>   as being in the presence of great people often does.

Well, I hadn't stopped to think how hard
>   climbing a tree in my robes would be;
>   >   or how undignified it probably was!
When I got up there, the first person I saw in the group with him,
>   was my dear friend, Levi.
This seemed to confirm I had done the right thing.
But imagine my surprise when Jesus stopped right under my tree,
>   looked me straight in the eye, and called me – by name!
"Zacchaeus, hurry and come down; for I must stay at your house today."
It was just like when he went to Levi at his tax booth.
Well, I nearly fell out of my tree;
>   but I managed to get down in one piece,

                with growing joy in my heart.
I was pleased to welcome him.
The crowd was not so pleased though!
"He's gone to be the guest of one who is a sinner."
        Someone said, in an audible gibe.
For a fleeting second, I thought about the last comment:
    "What's he doing here!"
            Well, now I knew; even if they did not!

I now understand that God's spirit spoke to mine in those moments.
Jesus did not just spend time with sinners;
    he wanted them to turn their lives around.
By asking to come to my house he wanted such a change;
    for by coming there I would make him ceremonially unclean.
I had to purify my property to prevent this.
So what I declared to him was not just a change of heart,
    but a way to make my property clean for him to enter.
"I will sell half my possessions and give the money to the poor,"
    I promised. "And anyone I have defrauded
        I will repay four times as much," I added.
The Law requires repentance be accompanied by restitution;
    this I was readily prepared to do, and more,
        for the load it lifted from my heart and shoulders,
           and for the hope of a better life.
Jesus called me the most beautiful name – "Son of Abraham!"
So he was acknowledging I too
    was a valued member of the Jewish nation
    to whom the promises of the Covenant applied,
        as much as to those who were clean and right with God.
For a moment I recalled what my name meant. "Pure or righteous."[4]
I had become anything but these. Jesus gave my name back to me.
He told me I was saved.
Then he added these wonderful words of reassurance:
    "The Son of Man came to seek out and to save the lost."

So, what happened next? I did not realise that from Jericho on that day,

---

4   Ibid. P. 927

Jesus was heading for Jerusalem. There he was eventually arrested.
He was accused falsely of many things.
Undoubtedly, one reason the religious leaders were upset with him,
    was that he willingly spent quality time with people like me.
He was executed!
But rose again from the dead on the third day!
This confirmed what I had come to know in my heart
    – he is the Messiah!

Apparently he had told his disciples he would rise again,
    though I doubt they understood this – I couldn't have!
He called for his followers to join him in Galilee.
So I sold the rest of my property to go and be with them[5];
    now many more than the twelve,
        which had become eleven, when Judas betrayed him.
I wasn't going to be able to get another job.
Now, I wanted his Spirit within me,
    so that I might tell about his great love for all people.

You see three things are certain in life!
    Taxes, death and the great love of God!
A love that he has even for the worst of us!
It is a love that transforms.
We can be reborn from the deaths we must die
    – and I don't just mean at the end of our lives.
We can be forgiven and freed – and I thank God that I know I am.

---

5 The idea that Zaccheus sold his remaining possessions and followed Jesus comes from Stuart Jackman, *The Davidson Affair,* Faber and Faber, London, 1966. Others, like Bartimaeus, having been healed, followed Jesus "on the way." (Mark 10:52) In Luke's Gospel, there are frequent suggestions that a growing number of people followed Jesus having heard his words and seen his deeds.

Jairus – A Leader of the Synagogue

(Mark 5: 21-43; Luke 8:40-56)

My name is Jairus.
As I am a leader in the Synagogue,
> it is very easy to suppose that what happened on the day,
>> for which I am most remembered,
>>> was all to do with my position.

That is, a Synagogue official coming to Jesus,
> who may be the Messiah, but certainly a faith healer,
>> expecting that because of my position
>>> he might do me a favour and heal my dying daughter!

Well, my friends, let me tell you,
> that is certainly not what it was all about.

I am a parent, a father! My daughter, my only daughter, was dying.
Twelve years old – about to come of age!
Do you understand how that made me feel?
You parents out there – how would you feel?
I was desperate!
My wife and I despaired greatly
and the possibility of our only daughter dying so young distressed us;
> as it would any parent!

Sure, a daughter in my culture is not treated as well as a son;
but she is my flesh and blood, and one does not dismiss this lightly.

And so I came to Jesus.
I do not even know who I thought he was when I came.
One thing I did know,
> was that I had heard stories of how he had healed people.

I was in such a state that I would have tried anyone
> I thought could heal her.

Believe me, it is no easy thing to come out into the public
> and humiliate myself in front of the crowds like that.

Yes, humiliate myself!
I, an official of the Synagogue, used to having people come to me;

       used to being the one in control!
You know how hard it was for me to be not in control for once?
People of my position do not normally go around in public
       throwing themselves at the feet of itinerant rabbis,
           beseeching a favour of faith.
That was very humiliating for me!
But a father will do even that for a dying child.
If I thought about it, I didn't really know what I was doing there.
Maybe at that point it was more hope than faith;
       or at the very least blind faith.

But then that woman interrupted Jesus as he went with me to my home.
The Synagogue official within me would say
that she should not even have been there in the midst of the crowd,
       potentially brushing up against people.
She was unclean, for crying out loud!
But then, I would not normally be there either!
Not because of uncleanness,
       but because I just don't mix with the crowds;
           - the ordinary people, that is!
Well, away from the Synagogue, at least!
When I "mix" there, I do it on my terms;
       and according to the Synagogue rules.
I certainly wouldn't come into contact with a woman like this.
That's the Synagogue official within me!
On that day, I was not on the street in that role.
I was there as a worried parent, concerned about my dying child.
And yes, of course I resented that woman's intrusion!
It was an interruption to Jesus' progress;
       a delay that ultimately cost my daughter her life.
But I realised that woman gave me a faith I came without!
I didn't know despair until I met her!
Twelve years sick,
       bleeding, unclean, and therefore ostracised!
Twelve years dead – or as good as!
She could have been my wife, bleeding since the birth of my daughter.
A daughter I now feared I would lose!

I had been in this concerned state only days, since my daughter fell ill.
This woman had lived with it like a growth in the gut,
      for twelve, frustrating, agonising years.

I had very publicly summoned Jesus to come and lay his hands
        upon my daughter.
This woman – because of who she was –
      could but secretly come and touch his hem,
          hoping, nay believing, she would be healed.
Like I said, this is the faith I came without.
I had come with hope: she had come with faith.
Simple, or as complex as that; take your pick.
Such was the power that flowed out from Jesus,
      through a mere touch of his hem, she was healed!
For all that flooded through me at that point,
      I knew that if this woman could be healed,
         so could my daughter.

And so moments later when messengers came
      to announce my daughter's death,
         I was torn apart.
But only momentarily, for he immediately urged me,
      "Don't be afraid, only believe!"
          And from somewhere deep within me, I did!
          Against all logic, I believed!
          Against all my teaching had told me!
          Against all the Synagogue stood for!
            I DID believe!

Jesus allowed only three of his disciples to come with us to my house.
Under any other circumstances, I may have protested.
Let this woman come too, something said within me!
But my mind was on other things;
      the adrenalin and this new faith-driven hope carried me home.
For some reason I sensed that she did not obey him;
      just as she had broken other rules that day.
I sensed she followed us.

If she did, I wonder how she felt when we were met
    by wailing mourners at the door.
When Jesus said my daughter was only asleep, they laughed!
If she was there, I am sure she would have words with them,
    when he sent them outside.

The rest is history! He raised my daughter from the dead.
    That day, two women gained new life!
        And my family was restored – reinvigorated!
Be assured that since then, we have grown close to that woman
    and spend days encouraging people to believe also.
Jesus told us to tell no one what had happened;
    but how could we keep something like this quiet?
Besides, the people were sure that my daughter was dead;
    how were we to explain that she was alive again?
No, we share our stories with whoever will listen;
    and even some who are reluctant to do so.
Our faith is in the mighty power of Jesus, the Son of God.
A faith I doubt the Synagogue could ever give me.
It came in the first instance from that woman – an uneducated outcast;
    and was verified by the Saviour we share, who rejects no one.
If only sharing stories
    like these could be the driving force of all
        we do in our community!
It would surely be quite a different place in which to live.

The Temptations of Jesus According to a Former Apprentice Devil

(Luke 4:1-13, 23:35[6] Ephesians 1:19-20)

I should have guessed I would have to hear that version of events.
You might accord a guest a little more respect.
No, I'm not the Devil – don't be foolish, woman
    (Addressed to no one in particular in the audience).
He wouldn't waste his time coming here.
Besides, you pay peanuts and you get monkeys!

No, I'm just an apprentice to the Devil. Well I was!
Confined to supermarket duties now!
What are they? Surely, everyone knows them or their effects!
    Wobbly wheels on trolleys!
    Nothing on the Specials shelves!
    Price Tags mixed up!
    Squashed fruit on the bottom!
        Where do you think they all come from?

It is 2000 years since I was demoted.
    Wasn't always supermarket duties of course!
First, it was the Colosseum.
Wobbly chariot wheels! Fixed gladiatorial games! Bent bookmakers!
You'd think I might at least have got Calendar Department!
Oh, come on, don't you know anything that's going on in the world?
How do you think St.Valentine's day falls in Lent so often.
All that chocolate to tempt, so early in the season!

But, no! A 2000 year demotion – that's what I got!
There is no forgiveness in Hell – you better believe it!
You see, I was assigned the job of tempting Jesus – ugh!
Oh, that name grates! It causes me so much anguish.
No wonder some people use it as a swear word.

---

6   There is an assumption (conveyed in the opening lines of this story) that if this story is told in a worship service, this passage will have been read beforehand.

That should have been an easy enough assignment
	– tempt a placid person like that.
So called – Prince of Peace – and all that!
Perhaps I was briefed wrong.
Or maybe, as I have been told a thousand times since, I just got it wrong!
He mightn't forgive, but the Devil is big on retribution.

Use the "IF" word – that's the basic principle, he told me.
You tell them how to get what they want and they always fall for it.
Look at Adam and Eve! We did that one well.
IF you want to be like God – and that is what you want, isn't it –
	then eat the fruit!
Fell for it, hook, line and sinker. See, we're into fishing for people too!

With Jesus- ugh! – it was different.
He was supposed to be God, right; yet he was trying to be truly human!
The Messiah, supposedly – but what sort of Messiah was he?
So, I had it worked out – question his divinity;
	ask him to do things I knew he could do,
	and that would have proven he wasn't human.
Look, I could have done him a favour – speed up his mission!
Here he was starting out on his goal to save the world.
I was offering him some panache! Some spectacle!
A way of getting the people in – attracted to the glitz!
Surely anyone in his position would give their right arm for that.
Let's face it; a job like that needed a good PR man.
I was him; that's why the boss gave me the task.
If you are God – I wanted to say to him – dazzle me, dazzle them!
	Win them over!
For example, create food on demand.
Even the Romans used to provide free food to the people.
That would have caught their attention. He could have done it!
I mean, didn't he later feed five thousand people
	with five loaves of bread?
And turn water into wine!
It was his scene. He could have done it.

Then I offered him control of the kingdoms of the world.
Wasn't that what he was working for, in his own pathetic way!
He could have had all this whilst protecting himself.
    He only had to worship the Devil.
Surely that wasn't too hard
    – there's people in the world doing it everyday, in their own way.
Of course, to be truthful, and I usually am not, there was no "only" to it

And then,
 because I knew God had supposedly promised to take care of him,
I wanted him to perform a little experiment that could show the world
    and prove to himself, that he really was invincible.
He could have shown he really was –
    the thundering, all-conquering Messiah,
        that the people were looking for.
He would have had them eating out of his hand.
He could have accomplished his mission in no time at all,
    and got back to where he belongs as quick as he liked.
You know, back to that other place he came from!
See, we were offering him
    something most people would find pretty enticing.
I know he didn't claim to be "most people";
    but he did want to be human.
Well, these are the things people want.
Here he was, wanting to convince people he was human.
 If he had what they wanted, they'd fall over themselves to follow him.
Jesus – ugh! – could have the good bits of being human
    without the other bits.
Nice food to eat without feeling hungry – and without the toil!
How does that sound to you?
Confront risks without any real danger. Bit of excitement in life!
Enjoy fame, wealth and power
    without the possibility of painful rejection.
I could have given him all this.
Wouldn't you think he'd be glad to have these
    and use them to his own advantage.
Lot less suffering for himself – and a lot less suffering for YOU!

And all the other humans in the world then and ever since!

You see, the power my boss is into is about coercion, and dazzle;
    forced obedience; loss of free will.
May not sound so good, but the benefits are out of this world.
Oh, and there's a bit of destruction. A few people will get hurt.
We call that collateral damage; don't you?
That's something we've taught a few world leaders
    pretty well throughout history.
You'd have to agree it's very effective.
Just look around the world today. Read your history books.
But God's power is not like that. It's more inside you! It's dangerous!
We can't get at people so easily when they are moved
    by things like – love!
But it can be rendered powerless when the one loved chooses to reject it.
We could have got somewhere with that if Jesus – ugh! -
    had accepted my offer to rule the kingdoms of the world.
In two of his tests I was merely asking him to prove himself.
But then, I overstepped the mark.
By seeking his worship,
    I was asking for something God would never allow.
So, I set the test, but in the end it was me who failed.
I still left feeling pleased that I had had a small victory.
You see, his refusal to play our rules,
    meant we could keep playing by them.
That wasn't the end of it. We did keep playing them!
They may not have been recorded in the same way.
Of course we had our human agents as well
    – two names that come to mind are Peter and Judas.
You may know some of their stories.
    Both in Jesus – ugh! – inner sanctum of believers!
One kept putting his foot in it,
    and eventually denied he even knew his master.
The other betrayed him into the hands of our human cohorts.
    How we got him on the cross!
We still had the kingdoms of the world – he turned down my offer.
And we learnt something about God's restraint,

which creates opportunities for those of us who oppose his kingdom.

We kept trying throughout his life. We even had him killed.
Remember that other famous "IF"?
It wasn't me, but as I heard it, I recalled my little battle with Jesus –ugh!
Recall those gathered at the foot of the cross
    when that fool got his just desserts.
        "If he is the Messiah, let him save himself!"
He could have.
    As I see it, he didn't have to die.
I could have prevented that three years earlier.
And he could have prevented it too!
But then he wouldn't have been our greatest –
    (*pause, awareness, deflated*) – defeat!
I was well off the case by then.
But you can be sure that the boss used all his power
    to ensure that there was no resurrection.
That is, to ensure the so-called Son of God, stayed dead!
Apparently, all our power wasn't enough.
Well, if you believe he really rose from the dead –
    and I for one have my doubts!
I guess I need say no more – especially amongst the likes of you!
It was really only after that event that
    I was struck off for my earlier failure!
The boss doesn't admit too much, but he took it pretty badly,
    and a whole host of his cohorts paid dearly.
There are plenty of scapegoats where I come from!

But be assured, the battle continues! And we have our victories!
You never know, you may just be part of some of them!
    I hope I see you around!
But if you don't, you might see where I've been.
I AM trying to get my job back – remember! I'll do whatever it takes!
So what are you putting your energies into?
Hope it is for the good – I mean, I hope it is something worthwhile.
Of eternal significance, I mean!
For now, I wish you – the worst of luck!

The Innkeeper of Jericho and other Eye-Witnesses from the Beginning

A Blind Man sees Jesus enter Jerusalem
Peace in the midst of turmoil
(Matt. 20:29-21:17, 28: 1-20; Mark 10:46-52;
Luke 19:39, 23:34, 24: 1-53; Phil. 4:7)

It is common knowledge that the other senses of the blind
    become more acute.
I have long known this but it was only when I became blind
    that I appreciated how keen, for example, my hearing became.
Yes, as you sit there watching and listening to me,
    you observe I am no longer blind.
You are right. So let me tell you my story…

How or when I became blind is unimportant.
When it did happen I continued to live in Jerusalem, my home town.
There I lived by begging, as I could no longer work.
In those days, in that culture, there was no welfare system,
    as your culture may be accustomed to.
If you could not work, you begged.
A good place for me to do this was at the main gates of Jerusalem,
    where travellers from places like Jericho would enter the city.
Here I could seek money from visitors to the city,
    rather than always relying on locals and those who knew me,
        who felt sorry for me because of that.

It was there that I sat one day just before the Passover.
For this reason there were extra visitors coming into the city,
perhaps to celebrate that Festival meal with family members and friends.
At the best of times the entrance to the city
    is a mixture of sounds and smells:
        of people coming and going;
            sellers and buyers at the stalls near the gates;
                beggars like me calling out for alms.
As one who was blind and sitting still,
I found it fascinating listening to the different voices and footsteps.

On this day, I heard approaching me,
        on the road from Bethphage that continues on to Jericho,
            a crowd of people shouting and cheering:
"Hosanna to the Son of David!
Blessed is the one who comes in the name of the Lord!
Hosanna in the highest heaven!"
It was adulation fit for a king;
      but the words suggested a religious leader,
        not a Herod, a Pilate or a Caesar!
I sat there wondering who this could be
      and what group it was that greeted him in this way.

As the shouting drew nearer,
        overshadowing the everyday sounds around me,
            there was a new sound; different voices.
It was as though others who were listening
     and those fortunate enough to be watching,
        began to express aloud what I was wondering to myself.
"Who is this?"
So I was swept up in a growing crescendo.
Behind me, echoes of "Who is this?";
     and others expressing their own answers to this question.
Ahead, approaching at a steady pace, a growing crowd sang
     "Hosanna to the Son of David!"
Within the crowd around me came the opinion that this was the prophet,
Jesus of Nazareth.
Some were clearly pleased; others were sceptical and critical of him.

Now, I had sat at that gate long enough to have heard
     many prophets and rabbis pass by,
       but none have received such a welcome.
From behind me were comments like: "He might be the Messiah."
Other voices there,
     and I recognised those of some of our religious leaders,
       rejected this outright, with mockery and cynicism..
One even told the rabbi to have his disciples "be quiet."

Then two strange things happened!
As the crowds merged into one – there was absolute turmoil around me.
But there was a peace
> that seemed to exude from the person at the centre of this uproar.
>> I could positively feel it!
Even amidst this turmoil, I could hear the clip clop of two beasts
> sounded like a donkey and a colt
>> – I gathered carrying this Jesus!
Later he would be executed!
As I reflected back to this moment after that tragedy,
> I realised he must have known what was to happen;
>> and I could only marvel that he was so peaceful and calm.
Indeed even entering the city
> he may have known what was going to happen;
>> and still he came.
This peace clearly came from within him,
> and seemed unaffected by the turmoil pressing in on him
>> and surrounding him.

"Who is this?" I said, asking my own question,
> but joining in with the crowd without realising it.
Now, the question did not mean what was his name;
> but what was this man, that had such an air about him
>> and affected so many people in so many different ways.
The question, though uttered aloud, was meant for no one.
A sort of out-loud wondering!
But a voice from a person standing very close to me spoke into my ear.
"The Messiah; God's own Son come to save us!"
And in the instant of those words,
> an arm linked to the voice, scooped me up.
>> "Come and meet him!"
>> "Who are you?"
>> "Bartimaeus, son of Timaeus, from Jericho.
>> "Do you know this prophet?"
>>> I already felt completely at ease with this stranger.
>> "Know him!
>>> He gave me back my sight. I was blind like you.

> Afterwards, I joined his group of followers
> and came with him here from Jericho."

That seemed to me a long story. I needed to hear some more.
But the surrounding noise was too loud to believe I would hear it told
even if I asked.
However, I trusted Bartimaeus, and his words gave me enough clues
to suspect, even dare to believe, what was coming!
I struggled at first to keep up with my companion;
but regained some composure when I realised
we were climbing a set of steps.
Grand steps!
I sensed they were the Temple steps.
I hadn't been up those steps since I became blind.
The sick, like other outcasts, being unclean,
are not welcome in most parts of the Temple.
Can you imagine how I have felt being excluded in this way
from practising religion, and branded "unclean"!
Besides, you will appreciate that steps are difficult for the blind,
unless they are guided.
I soon realised the sensitivity with which Bartimaeus led me.
A former blind person knows how to lead the blind!

As we neared the courtyard the surrounding sounds gave way
to those of the traders in the Temple courtyard.
Sheep; doves; voices haggling; money jingling
– all the familiar sounds of the market.
It is a recognised part of the Temple culture.
 But it is also a beat-up!
The priests and Temple authorities exploit people,
demanding they buy their sacrificial animals from the Temple
at their prices;
and by requiring the exchange of other currencies
for the offering at unfair rates.
Both enable them to charge so as to make large profits.
And they call this part of the practice of faith.

> In an instant these familiar sounds became a series of explosions
>> bursting round my ears.
>
> I realised that tables and chairs were being turned over,
>> smashing on the stonework.
>
> Money was splashing onto the ground and flying in all directions.
>> Had I been able to see I could have grabbed some
>>> as it passed my ear.
>
> Doves whooshed past my ear in a flurry of freed and flapping wings,
>> feathers flying freely!
>
> Released animals clattered across the stones, crashing into my legs
>> as they searched for an exit as quickly as possible.
>>> I could have caught one of them too!
>
> It sounded like Jesus was demolishing the Temple market.
> Then I heard his voice for the first time.
>> It was clear! It was angry! It was resolute!
>
> Yet still it sounded more composed than the turmoil around us.
> "It is written: 'My house shall be a house of prayer';
>> but you have made it a den of robbers."
>
> Again there was too much going on here for me to absorb it all.
> But two words struck me – "My house"!
> Who calls the Temple, "my house"?
> Was Bartimaeus right? Was this man laying claim to being the Messiah?
> My heart had been racing since Bartimaeus had taken me by the arm.
> The world all around me was racing also. And so were my thoughts!
>> Too much had happened all at once.
>>> I was almost thankful I couldn't see it all as well.

> But then, I was aware that Bartimaeus was still leading me.
> We had walked through the chaos of this Temple dismantling.
> The pandemonium unleashed by the market's demise
>> continued to burst around me,
>>> but was beginning to recede as I was glided away from it.
>
> I sensed we were entering another room
>> and being drawn into the presence of a small circle of peace.
>
> Once more it emanated from one person in the group,
>> and whilst there was chatter amongst others,
>>> even these were respecting the presence of this person.

I didn't need to know from whom. It had to be Jesus!
Bartimaeus spoke to him.
> "Teacher, let this man see again. Give him the gift you gave me."
> "Well, done my child." He said to Bartimaeus.
>> "Thank you for bringing him to me."

Then I felt his warm gaze upon me.
> "Son, receive your sight and go in peace."

My eyes were indeed opened. And so was my heart.
The first I saw was his deep warm eyes looking into mine
> – the mirrors of the soul.

I felt a peace within me that I could not understand,
> and the turmoil of the world,
>> of my world,
>>> seemed a long way away.

That peace has remained with me;
even though in the coming days, I watched with Bartimaeus,
> with our newly found sight,
>> when Jesus was cruelly executed.

At the foot of the cross, I wished I could not see again;
> and yet I knew the peace would remain;
>> a victory would be won. And it was!

That peace was what I sensed in Jesus,
> when he first passed me on the street.

It was the peace he must have had within him to be able to forgive those
> who drove the nails into his hands and feet.

It is the peace of God that is beyond all understanding.
> and I wish it upon you all
>> – and pray that the world may know it also.

Furthermore, they told me that he had prophesied
> that after his death he would indeed rise again.

Maybe that is why he had that peace.
And I thought at the time, "That's something I would like to see!";
> not thinking for one moment that I actually would see it.

But after what I had experienced, anything seemed possible.

A Blind Man sees Jesus enter Jerusalem

Still, I was amazed to hear, in the week after his death and burial,
        that he had indeed arisen and had been seen by the women first,
            then the disciples and other followers.
But then I quickly remembered that he was very much about new life.
Afterall, that is what he gave me!

The Innkeeper of Jericho and other Eye-Witnesses from the Beginning

Demos – former Jailer of Philippi

(Acts 16: 11-40; Philippians 3:1-7)

My name is Demos. They call me "The Captain."
I was once! A Captain in the Roman Army!
Now, I am an elder in the Church at Philippi.

Listen to what Paul wrote about us, in a letter to our Church.

I thank my God for you every time I think of you;
*   and every time I pray with joy*
*   because of the way in which you have helped me*
*   in the work of the gospel from the very first day until now.*
And so I am sure that God, who began this good work in you,
*   will carry it on until it is finished on the Day of Christ Jesus.*[7]

It is so humbling to have a man as great as Paul
praise us in this way.
I was there from very early.
Indeed I was Paul's third convert in this fine city of ours.
I remember it well, and it would give me great pleasure
    to share my story with you.

After I was pensioned out of the Roman army,
    I was posted here to Philippi, Macedonia,
        inland a little on the east coast of the Aegean Sea.
A long, long way from my home and friends!
But this has been my home now for many years
    – for it gave me a new life.

Let me tell you about this city,
for such information will help my story.[8]
It was named by Philip II, father of Alexander the Great.

---

7   Philippians 1:3-7
8   *The Interpreter's Dictionary of the Bible* Vol. 3 , Abingdon Press, Nashville, 1984   (14th Printing. First Published 1962) Pp. 786-7

The Innkeeper of Jericho and other Eye-Witnesses from the Beginning

He seized the gold mines nearby and turned
> what had been an enemy settlement
> into a stronghold for his own army.

Some years later in the third war between the Macedonians
> and the Romans, Rome took control of Philippi.

That was two hundred years before I came here.
Some famous battles have been fought here since then.
You may know of one of them.
It was here that Mark Antony and Octavian,
> who became Emperor Augustus, defeated Brutus and Cassius,
> > the assassins of Julius Caesar.

At that time army veterans were settled here.
More came later,
> especially after Octavian defeated Antony and Cleopatra here.

So like I said, famous battles of people you will know,
> have happened here.

Philippi has remained a Roman colony right through these years.
So, I guess I could have done worse when I left the army.
The injury that forced me out was only slight;
> but bad enough that they made me the local jailer.

They might at least have made me a lector
> – that's a police attendant of the magistrates.

They are at least lucky enough to see some decent action around town.

Life was hard here for me. Sure, I had a family, and I had a job.
And as a former soldier I commanded some respect.
> But I had been torn away from my home.
> I had lost my career as a soldier.
> I was confused about where life was taking me.
> I also had bad memories of the cruel acts
> > I had performed as a soldier.
>
> It went with the job. We all did as we were told.

But still I regularly struggled with my conscience trying to justify myself
> – what I had been!

Whether I had ever been successful?
I even sought the advice of a fortune teller.

I must have been awfully desperate!
Paid hard-earned cash to a slave girl, for a few answers,
    suspecting that it would probably end up in the purse
        of her selfish owners.
But I had to know!   Did life hold anything more for me?
Her predictions did give me some hope – without being terribly clear.
Maybe God worked through even the evil spirit
    who gave her that power; for it gave me the desire to know more.

    So when I wasn't working,
        I followed her in the hope of getting some further advice
          -   preferably on the side,
            without paying so dearly for it!

Soon after this I noticed her harassing some visitors from out of town.
Four of them there were
    – a couple of Jews, and two others who were Gentiles, like us;
        but I wasn't sure where they were from.
I noticed these things. The army had taught me to be observant.
Now I knew there were virtually no Jews living in Philippi.
Furthermore, I discovered these visitors were going off
    out to the riverside beyond the city walls,
        to take part in some sort of religious acts.
Well, that was what I had thought, then!
That small group of women that they prayed with,
    became the beginning of our Church here,
        and as unlikely as it seemed, I was soon to join them.

    But let me not get ahead of myself.
Although, I tell you this much,
    for my real attention was drawn to the slave girl fortune teller.
As I said, this drew me to these strangers, whom she began to harass.
She did so by saying something very strange to my ears.
She went around saying they were servants of the most high God.
These were words that I did not understand.
The Romans have their gods; and so do the Macedonians.
She seemed to be saying that there was one God

greater than any of these.
Yet it was generally acknowledged that her powers
    came from an evil spirit.
What kind of God could speak through such a spirit?
Here was more reason to question her.
Or them! But, I couldn't.
Instead, God brought them to me.

    She continued to say these things for many days;
        and they were clearly distressed by it.
Finally, one day, as I watched from a little distance,
    the leader of this group, a man I soon came to know as Paul,
        turned around to address her.
In his attack upon her, he shouted more words I did not understand.
    "In the name of Jesus Christ, I command you to come out!"
        Jesus Christ was a name we only knew as a legend
            from a far distant land.
I had met soldiers who had served in Israel, who saw him die.
    But they also said there were stories about him.
    That he was supposed to be a god,
    and that he rose from the dead after being executed on the cross.
To that day none of these stories had made sense to me.
But there seemed to be some connection
    between this most high God and this Jesus Christ.
The events that were unfolding before me,
    gave me no time to think any of this through.
        Even had I the means to do so.
Something happened to that girl – there and then!
It seemed that the spirit which gave her psychic powers,
    one we all believed was evil,
        left her immediately.
Now, I wasn't the only one who saw all this.
Nor was I the only one to whom it was quickly clear
    that she no longer had the ability to tell fortunes.
Her owners whom she had made rich,
    including with my hard-earned cash,
        were not too far away.

Not surprisingly,
    when they realised that their gold mine had been sealed up,
        they vented their anger on this group of strangers.
They seized two of them – the others fled –
    and dragged them before the magistrates.

To the magistrates, the slave girl's masters accused the Jews
    of being little more than vagabonds from out of town,
        who were pushing customs and beliefs
            that we Romans could neither accept nor practice.
At that point, in my ignorance, I could see their point of view.
Proselytization of Roman citizens by Jews
    was not actually illegal in Macedonia,
        but it was certainly met with strong disapproval.
Anyway, the magistrates were obliged
    to at least treat this as a disturbance of the peace.
Or that they were encouraging unlawful practices!
I could see that it was greed that motivated the accusations
    of these slave owners.
Nevertheless, they were respected citizens
    and the magistrates were not about to give
    any time to the pleas of some troublemakers
        who were foreigners, at that.
Besides, the crowd soon joined in, and they saw no reason
    why the magistrates should delay the exercise of justice.
Not that the magistrates in any sense investigated the claims.

The magistrates summoned their police
    to strip the strangers and beat them.
I grimaced as I watched –
    forgetting for a moment this was a job I had wanted;
    and forgetting also the far worse action I had seen as a soldier.
The Lictors, as these police were called,
    carried a bundle of rods that were a symbol of their position.
It was with these that Paul and his companion, Silas,
    were severely beaten.
Now, I was just a bystander.

Off work at the time, although I had a night shift ahead of me!
A magistrate saw me in the crowd
    and summoned me to throw them into prison,
        with strict instructions about how they were to be secured.
So my shift began early and naturally I did as I was ordered.
    A soldier always does!

They were dragged to the innermost cells of the prison.
This ensured the walls around them were not the outside walls.
    Their legs were placed in stocks.
        (Our stocks were designed to allow more than one pair of holes
        in a heavy block of wood.
        This meant the prisoner's legs could be
        spread apart into an agonising position.)
Thus, I left them – battered, bleeding and in ongoing pain.
I had other prisoners to attend to,
and so it was late that night before I could retire to my watch-house.
I was very tired and I had a lot on my mind.
These two prisoners were not what I was thinking about.

    As I settled down, I was then amazed to hear them,
        not groaning in their pain;
        nor fallen silent having passed out from that pain;
        but they were singing joyfully and talking to their gods.
            Or was it just one God?
As I strained to listen to them through the walls,
    I again heard those names: most high God and Jesus Christ,
        Son of that God.
How could they be so joyful in their strife and pain?
    What was it that drove them? I longed to go and question them.
    But as I struggled with my tiredness,
        their singing became something of a lullaby.

    I don't know how long I slept!
But it was apparently sometime after midnight
    that I was violently shaken awake.
An earthquake shook the very foundations of the prison.

The air was thick with the dust of the stone walls and floors!
>Every bolted door was flung open!
>The air cracked with the breaking of chains!

I now know that the one true God had acted!
As I rallied myself,
>I realised that the prison had been completely thrown open.

There was no chance that any of the prisoners would still be secured.
For such to happen – whether due to an act of the gods or of man –
>left me with no excuse for the loss of prisoners.

Realising the prisoners would all be gone, I determined to kill myself,
>rather than be subjected to the punishment I would surely suffer.

This state of mind followed quickly from the struggles
>I have earlier described.

It was almost a welcome and honourable "way out for me"!
Just as I was about to plunge my short sword into the base of my neck,
>a voice cried out from the darkness of the dungeon,
>>apparently aware of what I was about to do..

It was one of the foreign prisoners – Paul, the Jew.
"Don't harm yourself! All your prisoners are here!"
I couldn't believe my ears!
If this were the case, surely these men served a power or honour
>greater than I had ever known – even as a Roman soldier.

Overcome by a fear of an unknown,
>I procured a light and rushed to their side.

I was shaking like a man possessed by some sort of spirit.
I knew now that these men had something that I needed.
Not really knowing what I meant, I blurted out:
>"What must I do to be saved?"
>"Believe on the Lord Jesus Christ,
>>and you will be saved, and your family," said Paul.

There in that dark dusty hole, caked in blood and bruises,
>Paul and Silas told me about Jesus.

Deep inside me, I felt a release that I had never known before.

>I took them home.

Understand, I was not neglecting my duty in this,
>for they remained in my care.

I washed their wounds, with trembling hands, but a joyful heart.
And they washed me in the waters of baptism. I and my family also!
And the Spirit of the most high God filled our lives with a joy and peace
    that we had never known before.

    These men were released next day.
There was much fuss when it was discovered that although a Jew,
    Paul was a Roman citizen.
I brought them home again, and they told me about the band of believers,
      including a woman named Lydia,
          with whom they had been staying.
Later we met with her and the others for prayer and fellowship
    by the riverside.
Guess who was there?
The slave girl released from the evil spirit and from her fortune telling.
I did not have such a spirit,
    but I knew a release from all from the past that had bound me.
It was like Paul must have felt when his chains and stocks fell off.
Only, my chains bound something within me.

    And so the Church began in Philippi
      and we have never stopped praising God!

Philip's Nephew's Lunch
(John 6:1-2; Luke 8:1-3)

I didn't see my sister and ten year old nephew
        very often in those days.
Not since I had been travelling around the country with Jesus.
But I did see them soon after that day.
Although I thought I saw him in the crowd that day!
This was amazing given there were so many people there.
        Must have been well over five thousand people
                – if you count men, women and children!
                      (Which not everyone does!)

When I went to visit I soon discovered that
        "Yes!" it was him I had seen; talking to Andrew.
It'd been hard for Rachel, my sister, since she lost her husband;
bringing up her son on her own, and all that; so she relied on me a bit.
I didn't mind that because young Aaron was a great chap.
        A favourite nephew, really!
But as I said, I didn't get to see him often enough.

On this occasion, I had hardly arrived when she said,
        "Philip, I wish you would talk to Aaron.
                I can't cope with his stories. I just want the truth!"
"Why, what's he told you?"
"Well, yesterday he said he followed the crowds to listen to Jesus.
He's been all the talk since he has been healing sick people.
                Aaron was curious."
"I thought I saw him; but didn't get a chance to talk to him."

"He asked to take a packed lunch for himself and a friend.
        When he got home, his lunch was still in the bag;
                but broken in pieces.
        I asked him why he hadn't eaten his lunch;

and why he hadn't given some to young Joe,
      like he said he would.
He insisted they had had plenty to eat;
      but they couldn't have.
I'm not going to have him following around after Jesus
      if he's going to come home telling lies.
When I insisted he hadn't eaten his lunch,
      he told me a story too unbelievable for words.
            But he swears black and blue it's the truth."

"Well," I said,
      wondering when to tell her what I had seen happen,
      "what did he tell you?"
"Apparently, when the crowd were all gathered round,
      Aaron heard two of the disciples
            discussing how Jesus wanted to feed them all.
                  Five thousand you said!"
"No many more; if you count the women and children!"
"Exactly! So how unlikely is that for a start off!
      Where would you get enough bread to feed all them?"
"Funny you should ask!
      Jesus asked me the same question!
            Mind you, he told me this morning he was just testing me.
            He knew all along what he was going to do.
So to answer your question,
      I estimated more than two hundred silver coins.
            If all twelve of us pooled our resources
            we wouldn't have had more than a quarter of that!"
                  Even the resources of the women with us,
                        wouldn't have done it."
"What women?"
"I'll tell you about them later. Let's concentrate on yesterday."
"Did you see what happened after that?
      Or do I keep telling Aaron's story?"

      "I didn't properly see all that happened.
Jesus spoke to some of the other disciples,

Philip's Nephew's Lunch

and Andrew gave him a small bag of food."
"My smart-alec son reckons he offered Andrew the lunch
    I had packed for him –
        five barley loaves and a couple of dried fish!"
"Mmmmm, that could be right!"
"What! So you do know what happened?"
"This is what I thought happened! It was all quite amazing really!
    But after Jesus got a paralysed man up and walking the other day,
        nothing surprises me anymore."
"Philip, just one story at a time, please!
    That is hard enough, without more!"

"Jesus had this small bag of food.
I suppose it could have been Aaron's.
    Jesus told us to get the people to sit down;
        so I moved away doing just that.
I felt as if I had let him down with my answer about the money.
    I wanted to get something right.
I might have had my back turned to him for a moment,
    and when I faced him again, he was holding aloft
        about five loaves of bread, as if he were giving thanks to God."
"And two fish?"
"Yes, they came later."
"Perhaps it was Aaron's lunch!"

"He started to break the bread into pieces
    and give it to the lads to distribute amongst the people,
        who were sitting in groups by now.
I remember thinking,
'He's never going to feed all these people with that little pile of food.'
Then two miraculous things happened!"
    'Try me !'"

"I heard and saw a few people around me, doing the same thing.
    Sharing what little food they had with them.
It still wouldn't be enough, but they were following Jesus' example.
"Amazing! And what was the other thing?"

"Simon had half of one of the loaves from Jesus.
    He was quite near me;
    and he was tugging at the bread,
        almost willing it to go as far as possible.
            I tell you, I stood there watching,
                and the piece of bread wasn't getting any smaller.

    "Well, the people couldn't have got much each."
"They seemed to be quite adequately fed.
    I even had some afterwards myself and I certainly had plenty.
        Very nice bread, by the way!"
"Thank you! ... I mean, that sounds pretty extraordinary!" said Rachel.
    "And so, Aaron could have been telling the truth!
        Certainly, someone ate his lunch.
If it fed over five thousand people,
    then that must have been another sign from God.
        One thing it doesn't explain, though,
            is how come he brought home
        a bag full of broken pieces,
            as if he started eating and never finished."

"Well, you see there's more!
    When Jesus saw that everyone had had their fill,
        he told us not to waste any, but to gather up the scraps.
    There was more in that pile than what he started with."
"WHAT?"
"I reckon there were twelve baskets full left over.
    Whilst most of it went to the poor in the villages;
        I am sure I saw him shoving some back into the bag,
            so I guess it was given back to Aaron."

    "That's amazing!
        I must call Aaron and forgive him, for not believing him."
"You might also commend him for his faith." I suggested.
"Why?"
"Don't you see?
    None of us would have believed

    that so little food could feed so many.
 We would not have even bothered with such a small amount.
 But Aaron obviously believed Jesus could do something with it,
  otherwise he would not have offered it to Andrew
   in the first place."

 Then his mother showed me where this faith came from.
"I think there is more to this story than a simple miracle."
She said, pausing long enough to whet my curiosity.
"Jesus was determined right from the beginning to feed this crowd.
  He cared for them so much.
   His love for these people was so great.
    And like that small amount of bread,
     how far can even the smallest act of love go?
I think his love,
  like God has shown to us throughout the history of our people,
   is so great!
 It is bigger than we can ever comprehend;
 and yet he wants us to try and grasp it
 so that we can be completely filled with the nature of God.
That way we too can love people with all we have;
  even though it is meagre in comparison with God's love."

  I stood there stunned!
She walked towards the door.
  "Come on! Do you want some food?"
She said , and almost in the same breath she was calling her son.
  "AARON!"

---

† Again, I need to acknowledge that the core idea here was someone else's. Thomas Troeger, a professor of preaching and communications in Denver, Colorado, suggested it at a workshop I attended in Melbourne. I didn't hear him develop it as a story, but it percolated away in my mind and emerged some time later when I wanted to tell the story of the feeding of the multitude from a different perspective.

Many years beforehand I had seen a film about some Christian workers from Texas who crossed the border and worked with a group of poor Mexicans who gained a meagre income by combing the rubbish tips – for food and things they could sell. (The film's title is long forgotten.) One Christmas a special lunch was to be offered to these poor people; only for the workers to have more turn up than they had catered for. They decided to go ahead and hope to have enough for the people if the workers ate nothing. They were astounded to visibly see legs of ham not getting any smaller as they were carved with generosity. The workers were able to eat and afterwards there was enough left over to be taken into town to other agencies who worked with the poor. These images have remained vividly with me to this day.

Nicodemus – A Member of the Sanhedrin on the first Easter Day

(John 3: 1-21; 19: 38-43; Luke 22:3-6; 23:44-46, 50-51; Matthew 26: 14-16; 27:1-10; 62-28:15)

Nicodemus enters.[9]
His blood is on my hands!
Oh, how it stained my skin!
But it also scarred my soul!
I speak of Jesus' blood;
and I guess you are thinking that figuratively his blood is on us all!
He died that death on the cross for us all.
But I helped take him from the cross; that was the least I could do,
    especially when you realise that I helped put him on that cross.
My name is Nicodemus. You may have heard of me!
It was I who helped Joseph of Arimathea take Jesus from the cross,
    wrap him in a cloth with myrrh and aloes,
        and lay him in a tomb.

Oh, how the tears streamed down my face as we did this!
Our grief was so great!
Our tears were like his blood that streamed from gaping wounds.
    They mingled with that blood.
We were a sorry sight!
It was more complex than a doctor at an accident scene.
You see, touching the dead and the blood of the dead makes me unclean.
Do you understand what that means for me?
I am a Pharisee! A member of the High Court – the Sanhedrin!
A teacher of the Law and highly respected in the Temple.
We believe the law is strict,
    and all this means that I cannot even go into the Temple
        for a long time.
Yet, there is a sense in which his death has cut me free from all that.

---

[9] For all the pomp of his position, Nicodemus is wearing an outfit that is not that grand, but bloody though not outrageously so. This entrance is something akin to Lady Macbeth delivering her "Out, damn spot" speech. Yet here there is a sense of a restored assurance.

What I have done for him is the least I could do
    – given what he has done for me!
Somehow, the Law that has bound my life for so long,
    that has controlled everything I do – doesn't matter anymore!
I hear that when he died the grand curtain
    in front of the Holy of Holies in the Temple
        was ripped in two –   from top to bottom.
Have you seen that curtain! No human hands could have done that!
It is as though God himself was saying:
"Enough of your stupid religious games; all can come to me now!"

But let me return to what this all means to me.
Before a drop of his blood fell on me, I was already condemned.
I was on the Council that sentenced him.
I have never felt less comfortable in my life!
It was as though we were the ones on trial!
But I felt the guilt more than anyone else
    because I could see the gravity of what we were doing.
Joseph could too!
He was a member of the Council,
    and expressed his disapproval of the decision.
But why do I say I felt the guilt of that decision?
Because I believed in this man!
The evidence against Jesus was flimsy – we all knew that!
Had Jesus chosen to defend himself
    he could have wiped the floor with us.
But we were scared; scared of the people!
We were afraid that they might rally behind him against us;
    or bring the wrath of the Roman leadership
        crashing down upon us,
    even though we religious leaders enjoyed a good relationship
        with them.
I'm sure this may still come one day.
I was far from comfortable, but what could I do?
I was just one voice on the Council and a pretty pathetic one at that!
Joseph showed me up. Together, we might have been heard.
But I was scared too – though not like the rest of the Council.

Nicodemus – A Member of the Sanhedrin on the first Easter Day

I had to speak my mind,
    but to do so I risked being finished with the Council;
        ostracised by the High Priests;
        no longer respected as a Rabbi;
        frowned upon in the Temple.
I felt as though I had to think of myself and my future.
    Wouldn't anyone do the same?
But at least I wasn't facing a death sentence! Or maybe I was!

I failed him! I let him die!
I may not have been able to help Joseph persuade them,
    but at least I could have made my voice and feelings
        more strongly heard.   But no, I let him down!
It is cold comfort to know that even his closest followers did that.
And I can relate to their pain from doing so!
    They deserted him – in his time of greatest need!
    They slept – as he prayed!
    They ran away – as he was led away!
    Peter followed – but three times denied he even knew Jesus!
    Just as Jesus had predicted!
Three years they had been together,
    yet when he feared he would lose his life,
        Peter said he didn't even know him.

And what of Judas!
I was there when the Council met with him.
    He betrayed his own master for a lousy bag of silver!
I'm not really surprised he took his own life;
    knowing how I feel about what I did.
When Judas realised what he had done, it must have crushed him.
I could see it in his face when he threw the money back in our faces.
    Blood money!
"I have sinned by betraying innocent blood!" he cried out.
    Perhaps I should have gone after him.
        I might have saved one life.
I felt as guilty as those disciples.
The least I could do was bury Jesus; whatever the consequences!

From long ago I had agonised over who he is.
I had heard much about him. I had even heard some of his teachings.
So I went to him one night. I had to go! I had to go at night!
    "Rabbi", I said, "we know that you are from God.
        The signs you do could only be done by one
            in the presence of God."
One in the presence of God! He lived so close to God!
Now, I do believe that he is the Messiah – but not then!
How demoralising it must have been for him to be on that cross.
Knowing who he was and that he was right!
Yet deserted by his friends; and seemingly deserted by his God!
I was at the cross! I heard his cry:
    "My God, my God, why have you forsaken me?"
I wonder if he actually died of a broken heart,
    more than the wounds inflicted upon him.

That night I spoke to him, I didn't really understand what he was saying.
He spoke of new life, of being born again!
I could only think of physical birth; so this made no sense to me.
He spoke of the Spirit – God's Spirit!
He spoke of the wind,
    which we hear without knowing where it comes from!
I felt as if many years of learning and study of the Law were…
    just a nonsense!
All this study seemed to be of no help to me at all!
I was completely lost, and he was right to express surprise at this.
In fact I think my education made it too hard for me to accept!
My brain wouldn't let my heart and soul engage!
It was as if this head knowledge had closed down my feelings
    and my ability to exercise faith.
I thought I knew what was true – but seemingly only from the neck up!

Well, I'll tell you something!
I certainly felt something on that day before the Sabbath!
My heart was aching as I took him down from the cross.
I wasn't even thinking about the consequences

of the Law and religion for me
>for carrying a dead and bleeding body.
It was not like carrying the burden of the Law
>that I had dragged around for years.
Here in my arms was the most precious human being
>I had ever been near.
It was not the burden that I carried; it was who I was serving in that act.
It was the least I could do, after what he had done for me.

But why am I bereft!
This day should be a day of rejoicing, for I hear that he is alive!
>Not that I understand this!
The women went to the very tomb that Joseph and I had laid him in.
The last we heard the Romans had placed the governor's seal
>on the stone and posted armed guards.
I was not present when my colleagues demanded this of Pilate,
believing claims he would rise would lead to the theft of the body.
Nevertheless, when the women got there, these were gone!
>The tomb was open and empty!
The blood-stained grave clothes lay there empty.
And then he appeared to some of them!

I guess some of you will be like me!
All this is hard for me to comprehend;
>especially for one so dependent on the Law for so long,
>>where there are rules for every aspect of life.
But nothing to explain dead men rising!
I am an educated man!
I can't wrap my brain or learning around a resurrection.
But then I have had that problem before, as I have already confessed.
That night I met him, he spoke of new life.
It is only by faith, not through my wisdom or knowledge,
>that I could ever accept that Jesus is alive again!
Unless I am lucky enough to see him myself!
Many no doubt won't, and they will have to rely on faith.
I guess it was my faith he was encouraging me to use on that night.

Wait! I see now that it is as if my old life is dead!
Because he is alive, I have a new life!
A life now centred in Jesus the Christ, and not on the Law! He is my life!
For I have been born again, just as he said on that night I went to him.
But it was only when I grappled with his death and now his new life,
    that I could accept in my heart what he was offering me.
I can be born again! I have been born again!
It is nothing my head knowledge can help me with,
    for God has changed my heart!
What a day to begin this new life!
The day my Lord defeated death, and returned to life!
And I can say "Alleluia" to that! Can you?

Rich, Black, Outcast, 'Half-Man'

(Acts 8:26-40)

If I had chosen my own name, it would be something that means "try harder"; because that is what I have been telling myself my whole life. "Try harder, Try harder, you are not good enough!"

I didn't get to choose what I would be. Sadly, I am not alone in the world there. When I was a baby my parents had me castrated. They weren't being mean; just trying to guarantee me a place in life. That is, a job working in the royal palace, where they hired castrated men to do jobs like guarding the harem. So I'm grateful to them; and I am angry with them. I hated them for it. You see, when my teenage years came along, and my friends found their voices dropping and their parents talking marriage; my voice stayed high and my parents were saying, "No you cannot be married for you are different to the others!" And my friends sniggered at me and taunted me, "Yoooo-nuck! Yoooo-nuck!"

The only thing I knew was to try harder; to be a better scholar, to excel at everything – be more capable, more responsible, more successful. I was therefore a model teenager. It worked. I became a guard of the harem, as my parents had foreseen; and soon I was the chief guard. Because of my education, before I knew it I was Chancellor of the Ethiopian Treasury. In charge of all the royal wealth! But it was never enough! People feared me; but nobody loved me. I seldom got invited to social functions; when I did, the men especially, found me embarrassing. The women had no time for me at all. Sometimes I heard comments like "half a man" and "he's a freak." So I tried even harder to get respect and popularity; perhaps even to win some friends. The Queen sent me on diplomatic missions to Egypt, to the Nabateans, to Damascus. Every place I went, I learnt all that I could, especially about their gods. But nowhere, it seemed was there a god for a 'half man' like me. A eunuch! Nor, in some places, for a black man, like me!

Once, the Queen sent me to Jerusalem on diplomatic business. There I visited the Jewish Temple – a magnificent building. But divided into sections for different people, and I soon discovered I was pushed to the margins – again. As a Gentile I could only enter the court of the Gentiles, where the traders sold their sacrificial animals, and currency for the offering was exchanged at high prices. And as one who had been mutilated there were any number of people ready to point out that according to the Jewish scriptures, I was disqualified from full involvement in the Temple practices. Nevertheless, I read their scripture scrolls that told of a God that led them out of slavery in Egypt. A very different kind of God to others I had read about; one that actually cared about people. The Hebrews had a prophet named Isaiah. I bought the scroll he wrote. The priest who sold it to me had to check whether it was legal to sell a Hebrew scroll to a black foreigner. It was; if the black man paid 3 times the going rate. I paid, because I could, and because I really wanted that scroll. This Isaiah seemed to prophesy a coming ruler; a leader who would be a servant; who would earn the right to lead through suffering with the hurting people of the world. A most unusual prophecy; but I found my heart warmed as I read the scroll. Clearly I identified with those who suffered. After all, though I was strong, powerful, rich – I was only 'half a man', and ostracised for it.

As I bumped along the road in my chariot, returning home to Ethiopia, I was reading my scroll, "Like a sheep he was led to the slaughter, and like a lamb silent before the shearer." I had to laugh. That was me all right. I was six weeks old when they cut me. You can cry; but you can't protest, at that age. And I have been crying ever since. I read on, "In humiliation, justice was denied him." "Is this Isaiah talking about me or what", I wondered almost aloud.

At that point, I looked up and saw a man walking along beside my chariot. Well half jogging really, to keep up; and smiling at me.
"Do you understand what you are reading?" he asked.
"No." I said. "I haven't the faintest idea, although I can relate to it. I need someone to help me. Can you?"
"Yes," said the man, whose name I discovered was Philip. So I invited him onto my chariot.
"Who is this that Isaiah is writing about? Is he talking about himself or someone else? It almost seems like he is talking about me.
"May I tell you a story?" Philip asked. Then for an hour, or two or three, beginning with the words of Isaiah, he talked to me about a man named Jesus. A Jewish teacher, of humble beginnings, who seemed to reach out and touch all the hurting people – tax collectors, prostitutes, widows, lepers, foreigners. And I imagined people like me.
"The Jewish religious leaders worked with the Romans to have him killed. They accused him of sedition. Had him crucified!" Philip paused..

"I'm not surprised," I said sadly. But it was not the end of the story, as death normally is.

Philip continued and spoke of Jesus rising from the dead. This Jesus was the Messiah sent from the God the Jews worshipped, and of whom Isaiah wrote long before these events. One who came to serve the weak and the lost people, who no one else generally cared about.

Tentatively, I asked the question that had been on my mind for much of the Jesus' story. "Would Jesus care about me?"

"Of course!" Philip said, in an almost matter-of-fact sort of way.

"Did you know I was a eunuch?"

"I guessed. But why should that make any difference?"

I ignored the question, because he seemed not to get it. I went on ticking off my normal checklist,

"I'm black. I'm a foreigner. But I'm successful in people's eyes, for I am rich."

"That is all pretty obvious." Philip laughed. "But these sorts of things are of no concern to Jesus or to God. God is only interested in what is in your heart. God loves you. He doesn't care about your genitals; or your skin colour; or your nationality. He certainly doesn't reject you for being successful or wealthy; though he is interested to see what you do with these things."

It is a long time since I wept like I did that afternoon. Great tears fell as I felt a great weight lifted off my shoulders and falling by the wayside. Now, I really could stop trying harder, and concentrate on more important things. I was a real man, because I was loved by a real man, named Jesus, who even cared for eunuchs and foreigners. He died for me; rose again; and danced with his people.

My chariot was moving past a water hole by the roadside, and I recalled mention of baptism for the forgiveness of sins.

"There's water here, Philip! Can I be baptised?"

"Yes! Yes! Yes!" he replied emphatically.

I felt like I was under the water for an eternity; but it was a glorious eternity, when I felt my old self and all my fears and pains, dissolved into the water. And when Philip lifted me up, I felt I was a new person – a whole person. No longer incomplete in any way! I stood there in the warm spring air, beaming and thanking this new-found God, or rather who had found me. And I knew that everything had changed because of what Jesus had done. No longer did it matter what other people thought of me; only what he thought of me. I was a new being; in the same body, yes, but no longer needing to be ashamed of myself, because that was not how he saw me. God and his Son loved this body, and loved me – unconditionally – even if and when I didn't try harder. I had nothing more to prove.

"I can never thank you enough, Philip." I said turning to face him. I knew I would be eternally indebted to him. But he was gone! Nowhere to be seen; although I looked in every direction! Later I would understand that the Spirit had taken him to help another person somewhere else, who needed to hear what I had heard.

I sprang back onto my chariot, praising God.

"Let's go home," I shouted. "I have great news to share with the Ethiopians!"

The Writer of Mark Contemplating the Writing of a Gospel

(Based on various stories from that Gospel as we now have it.)
'Mark' enters with a scroll and quill.
    It seems to me that it is time.
A full account of the good news about Jesus the Christ
    must be written down.
It is quite some years since he returned to heaven,
    after his rising and before the coming of the Holy Spirit.
Still there is no complete record written down –
if there could ever be a full record.
Many have told the stories; and I write now,
    expecting this to be a collection that can be told
        in marketplaces and in other places
            where followers and inquirers gather.
There have been a few small collections made of the stories about him,
    but I doubt any of them will last as they are so incomplete.
I'm sure there will be others to follow.
There are so many stories, and no collection will be complete,
    for he met and touched so many people,
    and each collector of stories
        will see them fitting together differently.
I have noticed this myself when I have heard different eye-witnesses
    telling the stories of Jesus.

    I have gathered many of my stories from Simon Peter.
Mind you Paul has told me a few too,
    but he's got them from others because he wasn't a believer
    when Jesus was here.
I'm only sorry I wasn't around to know Jesus personally myself.
But being the first to make such a collection will be my contribution
    to the Kingdom.
Not that I expect to be remembered personally.
One day, they may even question who it was
    who actually made this collection.

    Anyway, it is time to get down to it.

I want to emphasise Jesus' true identity – Son of God, the Messiah -
    a Saviour whom Jews had waited for over many centuries.
My collection of stories of him can support that
    and build on knowledge of who he is.
I don't think I even want to be concerned with his earthly family
    or heritage.
So – no family tree! No birth stories!
    I haven't met Mary, but I hear her story is really very special,
    and I am sure someone will one day record it for all to know.
I want to start when his work begins. I think he was about thirty by then.

    Let me see.
(Writes and reads as he does so.) "The beginning of the good news…"
(Leaves off)
Evangelion – I love that word!
    The Good News – that's what it is all about.
"The beginning of the Good News of Jesus Christ, the Son of God."
    I like that!
This leaves no doubt as to what I'm on about.
What I want to achieve with my story collection, my narrative!
That is, who Jesus is! The Messiah! The Son of God!

    As I said, the stories will build on that.
God's voice from heaven at Jesus' baptism:
"You are my son, the Beloved, with you I am well pleased."
Then Peter's story about when they were in Caesarea Philippi,
    and Jesus asks:
        "Who do the people say that I am?"
And Peter identifies him as the Messiah!

    Then I think soon after that I'll include the story on the mountain,
        with Peter and some of the others,
            when Moses and Elijah appeared there with them.
Again the voice from heaven: "This is my Son, the Beloved."

    There was the healing of Bartimaeus, the blind beggar.
He called Jesus, "the Son of David."

That's an important title! That'll identify his heritage.
I want to put that right before the record of him going to Jerusalem
before his death.
And then I can end his crucifixion with that electric moment
when the Roman centurion identifies Jesus at the point of his death:
> "Truly this was the Son of God."

I would never have believed it was a Roman, if they hadn't told me.
Although I know many Romans with faith now!

I'm getting ahead of myself a bit here. What have I written down?
"The beginning of the Good News of Jesus Christ, the Son of God."
Is that all? I feel as if I have been writing for ages.
But then I forget. It is about telling the stories.

    Now, I think a prophecy from our scriptures that will introduce
some of the themes of Jesus' ministry;
    before I introduce John the Baptiser.
(Writes) "As it is written in the prophet Isaiah." *(Stops)*
Wait a minute!
I better be sure there is something from Isaiah that will say what I want.
I'm sure the Spirit of God will give me something.
I feel the inspiration of that Spirit very strongly as I write this,
    just as the apostles have in their ministries
        since the Spirit came upon them.

    What do I want that prophecy to say about Jesus?
Well, he is the messenger sent by God to sow the word
    – the Word of God.
Yes!
And there's that wonderful parable Jesus told about the sower
    going out to sow his seed.
That seed was the Word of God!
And the parable was about how the seed fell on different types of soil,
    who are the hearers that receive the word differently.
It is not too hard to see who they were as Jesus taught the people.
The stories are about these different types of hearers
    – how they responded to him.

I want to make that parable an important one in my collection.
So that's the first thing – he is the messenger sent by God.
He is also the message itself.
> I'll keep that in the back of my mind.

> Then he calls people to follow him on the way to Jerusalem
>> and the cross.

Well, he certainly told them he was going to suffer much and die;
> not that they understood.

But he also called them to follow him.

The voice of one crying in the wilderness;
> there's plenty of stories I can use here.

He was tempted in the wilderness.
He prayed and taught his disciples
> in the deserted places of the wilderness.

People followed him out into the wilderness
> and were taught and healed there.

It was in these deserted places
> he provided food for many from very small resources.
>> Fed a multitude with one person's meal!

So he performed miracles in the wilderness.
> There are lots of stories there I can use.

So Jesus seems to me to have been a voice: "Crying in the wilderness!"
But that also describes John as well.

So what's the prophecy I want to quote.
Let me see, I need to put something together here:
(Writes) "Behold! I am sending my messenger ahead of you,
> who will prepare your way:
> the voice of one crying in the wilderness:
> Prepare the way of the Lord, make his paths straight.'"

> Mmmmm! That's not actually all from the prophet, Isaiah.

I think there's a bit from Exodus. Some from the prophet, Malachi, too!
I should check that out. Never mind, they'll work it out!
Hearers will know the stories of their scriptures.

The Writer of Mark Contemplating the Writing of a Gospel

> They'll see what I've done.

Can I still write: "As it is written in the prophet Isaiah"?
It is a bit messy to mention all the bits separately.
I'll leave it like that for now and if I can find a different way to put it,
> I'll change it later.

> And so we get to John the Baptiser, and through his humanness,
>> introduce more about who Jesus is.

John calls the people to repent
> and be baptised for the forgiveness of their sins.

But it is interesting about John that his appearance points
> to a fulfilment of a promise of old.

He wore a camel skin, a leather girdle, and ate wild honey and locusts.
Same as Elijah!
I wonder if they will pick up that connection?
You see there was an expectation that Elijah would return
> before the Messiah came.

But was it before he came in glory?
There is the mountain story, I said I want to include.
Elijah appeared then, and Jesus was yet to have his victory.
Albeit on a cross, when he did!
Surely I don't have to spell out how Elijah fits in. It will get too wordy!
I want to be precise and to the point, bouncing from one story to the next
> and leaving the people to make these sorts of connections.

They know the stories!

> Of course, the Elijah connection
>> comes up again at Caesarea Philippi.

"Who do people say that I am?"
"John the Baptist! Elijah or one of the prophets!
Oh! I love these stories; they just all fit together. God's great jigsaw!
Umm! Have we got jigsaws yet? Not sure.
> Maybe I just invented a word; an idea.
>> God's great jigsaw!

> Then I need to say that John recognises and tells the people
>> that he is not the one who is to come –

that is, the Messiah!
"I have come," he said,
　　"to baptise with water, but he will baptise with the Holy Spirit."
And then at his baptism,
　　the Spirit descends upon Jesus in the form of a dove.
Probably no one realised at the time what was happening.
But Jesus is the Spirit's man! God's man – God's Son – in Galilee!
His ministry is animated by the very breath of God.
That is why I want to get so quickly into the stories of his ministry.
He is the life-giver,
　　and so I want to get straight into some of those stories
　　　　where he gives new life to people.
The healings, the exorcisms, the miracles!
Oh! I'm going to love writing these stories down,
　　just as storytellers love to tell them,
　　　　and people are blessed when they hear them.

So I begin with a trumpet call; I want to portray a Jesus who announces:
　　"I am the Christ!
　　I am the Messiah!
　　 I come to bring God's eternal kingdom to you.
　　I come to bring peace and hope."
And there is an urgency about the proclamation!
I want to reflect that urgency in the style of my writing,
　　moving quickly from one story to the next.
Introducing them with *"Kai Euthus!"* "And immediately!"
One story after another – Bang! Bang! Bang!
As if Jesus hardly has time to draw breath!
Hopefully, neither will my readers, and those who hear the stories told.

　　I want them, over however many years my record lasts,
to hear these words with fear and astonishment – and that urgency!
And to be convinced by the trumpet call of these words!
So I hope the Holy Spirit will empower us all
　　to believe the word of this Messiah.
This so that we too will spread the Good News to all whom we meet!
Perhaps I should end with that encouragement.

The Writer of Mark Contemplating the Writing of a Gospel

What if I suggest the resurrection
    but not have detailed appearance stories!
Then I can encourage the hearers of these words to share them
    with others ; what Jesus did and therefore who he is!

    I'll have to think more about that. It is a very big idea to end with.
However, I want it to fire people up to go out
    making the kind of proclamation
        my whole book tries to make through Jesus.
But now, if you will excuse me,
    I need to go and tidy up this section and get on with my writing.
In the meantime,
    I urge you to remember my words from God to you today
– and tell others!

The Innkeeper of Jericho and other Eye-Witnesses from the Beginning

A Nazarene Jew who found a New Faith

    This last five years or so have been pretty amazing really.
I mean, what I have seen and experienced has been –
        beyond human comprehension.
It has meant seeing God, whom we call Yahweh, in a new way,
        and that in itself was not easy for a Jew.

    Bear with me, and I will tell you the story from the beginning.
I was in my late twenties when I heard the preaching of John;
        they called him the Baptist or the Baptiser.
Fiery preacher, he was!
        "Prepare the way of the Lord!"
Later, "You brood of vipers,
            who warned you to flee the wrath to come?"
He sounded a bit like one of the old time prophets from years back.
Anyhow, I accepted his call to turn from my wrong ways
        and be baptised.
"A baptism of repentance for the forgiveness of sins", he called it.

    John was such a dynamic personality,
you had to wonder if he was –
        could he possibly be ? The Messiah!

    Well, he answered that himself:
"I baptise with water,
        but one is coming who is more powerful than me.
He will baptise with the Holy Spirit and with fire!"
        That was pretty scary stuff!   The breath of God, hey!
            I determined to watch out for this person.

    Well, I didn't have to wait long.
I went done to the River Jordan on another occasion,
        to hang around and listen to John preaching.
While I was there, Joseph's son, Jesus
        -a carpenter like his father –
            came to be baptised.

I'd known Jesus for a few years – we were teenagers together. He was older than me though
- about thirty when all this happened.
He was a great guy,
but not what you would call a dynamic personality.

Anyway, when he came to John,
I thought I heard John say he wouldn't.
Baptise him, that is!
Something about it not being right for him to baptise Jesus!
Those of us who heard it, were a bit puzzled by this.
It didn't seem like John to refuse anyone, like that.
But Jesus persuaded him to do it.
As he was coming up out of the water,
I swear I saw a white dove come down.
It seemed to come from nowhere and hover over Jesus.

Then another strange thing happened.
There was thunder in the sky,
even though there wasn't a storm cloud to be seen.
But then I swear I heard a voice.
Others there say "no!" But some agreed with me.
Something about Jesus being "a Beloved Son,"
with whom the speaker was pleased.
I have spoken to some of the followers
who have been telling the stories of Jesus,
and they say that's what they were told
by various members of the crowd.

It was like it was the very voice of Yahweh – God!
But that couldn't be – we argued –
because that would make Jesus,
Joseph's Son ...
... the Son of God !
The Messiah!
But we all knew Mary and Joseph?
I had difficulty with that – then at least.

But certainly, Jesus was a changed man.
He seemed to be overcome by some joyous, power-giving spirit.
Could it be the "Breath of God" that John had spoken about.
"One is coming who is more powerful than me.
He will baptise with the Holy Spirit."
Of course, I didn't make this link until someone later made it.

Then Jesus marched off purposefully – into the wilderness!
Almost as though he had a prearranged meeting with someone!
Or as though he was being driven by some inner
– or outer – invisible force!
What a strange place to go!
Well, no one heard from him for about six weeks, I suppose.
He had taken no provisions – just the clothes he stood in.
Some of us wondered if we would ever see him again.
Crazy to go out there, alone, and unprepared!
All that promise gone!

But a friend of mine saw him come out of the wilderness
-when he eventually did!
He said Jesus was just as bold as when he'd gone in.
Albeit pretty shabby – and thinner.
But he seemed in really good spirit! There's that word again!
What did John mean by him baptising by the Holy Spirit?
Is that what happened to Jesus himself?
I was determined to hear more.

And hear more I did.
He started to teach in the synagogues;
and all of us who heard him were amazed at what he was saying.
This wasn't the carpenter son of Mary and Joseph, we'd grown up with!
Something had changed – mightily!

I was home in Nazareth, visiting the family, and I attended
the synagogue, as usual.
Jesus was there!
They asked him to read from the scriptures!

He turned to the scroll of the prophet, Isaiah.
He seemed to look for a particular place
    -or jump around a bit!
    Or not read all of it,
        as though he knew exactly what he wanted to say!
Anyway, this is what he "read"
    (or perhaps he recited it, though the scroll was there):

> *The Spirit of the Lord is upon me,*
> *because he has anointed me to bring good news to the poor,*
> *He has sent me to proclaim release to the captives,*
> *and recovery of sight to the blind,*
> *to let the oppressed go free,*
> *to proclaim the year of the Lord's favour.*

There it was again – "the Breath of God!"
We all knew the passage, of course –
    although what he read wasn't quite what we recalled.
We did recall in the past that we had wondered whether it referred
    to the Messiah
        -as many passages in our scriptures did.

    We waited for him to teach.
He just rolled up the scroll; returned it; and sat down.
    Still a sign that he might teach; as our rabbis sit to teach!
We waited!
Then he said, quite calmly, quietly, and almost matter-of-factually,
    "Today this scripture has been fulfilled in your hearing."

    Well, the scene all unravelled from there.
Some spoke well of him – but queried that this was Jesus, son of Joseph,
    whom we all knew. "How is HE speaking thus?"
Others grumbled
    because he had left from his reading reference to "vengeance"!
        Vengeance was important for ancient Jews.
Then he acknowledged that they might be looking
    for something special in his home town.

He had already been teaching in Capernaum.
But he referred instead to two stories from our Scriptures.
    Each referred to times of the prophets, Elijah and Elisha ,
        when Gentiles were the recipients of God's favour.
"No vengeance?" "God smiling on the Gentiles!"   This was too much!

    In no time, many in the synagogue were hustling him
out the door, to the brow of the hill, on which the town stood,
    ready to throw him off the cliff!
Somehow, he calmly walked through their midst and went on his way.

    I held back. Wondering!
We have had false Messiahs before.
    Here was a man I had known for years,
        claiming to have the Spirit of God.
    I admit, I was beginning to be convinced.
        But the proof had to be in what I did next, I thought.

    So, over the next months, I followed him as much as I could.
And I saw astounding things!
    Those words of Isaiah came true before my very eyes!
        Blind people were given their sight back!
        The lame walked!
        Lepers were healed and freed of the oppressive life
            of outcasts!
        Demons were cast out! The possessed were freed!
        Yes, people bound up by all sorts of evil and illness,
            were released!
        Even dead people were raised!

    And I knew that this Jesus really had God's Spirit!
He must be the Son of God!
    The Messiah!
    Not that I understood all that this meant.
I became one of his regular followers.
    Not one of his chosen twelve, mind you.
    And secretly!

I wasn't sure what might happen had I professed it openly.
It was clear from that day in Nazareth that there was opposition to him.
Increasingly, over the next couple of years, whilst followers grew,
    so did opposition against him.
    The Pharisees, teachers of the Law, and the Temple Leaders,
        were not too happy.
    About him!   About the following he was gaining!

    Eventually, the bottom seemed to fall out of it all, rather quickly!
Just before one Passover,
    he rode into Jerusalem to a tumultuous welcome.
A few days later, he was arrested on some trumped up charges;
    the religious leaders having gained support
        from the very crowds that had greeted him,
            and more importantly from the Roman governor!
        He was sentenced to death!

    Knowing how bitterly disappointed I was,
I can imagine how confused his disciples must have been.
    I mean, I know now that we misunderstood a lot of things he said.
Nevertheless, we really felt, as he hung on that cross,
    that it may have been all some sort of fairy tale
        that had come to anything but a happy ending.
    Could this possibly be all there was?

    But, no, that wasn't the end of it. Far from it!
A few days later I heard he'd risen from the dead.
I, like others, had gone back home to nurse my grief.
    We were all a bit worried there would be a purge
        and anyone who'd been seen with him
            would be rounded up and strung up like him.
When I heard that he had been seen alive again, I was flabbergasted!
    Well, overjoyed, yet still confused.
        But then, I suppose he had raised others from the dead.
Apparently he had told the twelve this was going to happen.
    But like I said there was a lot we all didn't understand; until later!

I wondered what would come next.
Was he going to stay for a long time?
    Surely he couldn't just pick up where he had left off.
        Can a person die twice?
            He was clearly alive, but not the same as us.
About six weeks later, he disappeared up into thin air,
    in front of his disciples.

We were still confused.
Even those close to him, like the disciples and the women!
    I mean, he said all sorts of things.
    He made all sorts of promises,
        but we couldn't really comprehend them.
    What we could do was what he told us.   Wait!

One day, on the day of the festival of Pentecost,
there were over a hundred of us meeting and praying and waiting
    -not all that sure what we were waiting for!
The stories had got too much for me, and I had returned to Jerusalem.
    I wasn't alone in doing this!
He had talked of sending the Spirit, and that sent me, for one, scurrying,
    to recall those early days when I first met him.
        The baptism! The wilderness! The reading in Nazareth!

Suddenly, as we gathered together,
    we heard the sound of a rushing wind,
        as if we were on a hill, but we were inside.
We heard it, but it didn't blow us about!
Then we saw flames of fire, resting on each others' heads!
    But our hair wasn't singed or burnt!
    Now I knew, as if something had suddenly been revealed to me,
        that we were having an experience,
            like the one Jesus had three years earlier.

    The Spirit John had spoken of!
The Spirit that seemed to descend upon Jesus at his baptism!
The Spirit Jesus had read about from Isaiah!

The Spirit Jesus himself seemed to be empowered by!
    It was coming into us!
We were bold! As he had been when he marched into the wilderness.
    We had new gifts and powers;
        that we soon discovered enabled us to do a ministry like his.

    Since then, the number of followers has grown,
by the hundreds and by the thousands.
    Three thousand on that first day alone!
        Spread all over the world; and amongst the Gentiles even.
I would never have believed that possible.
    But I guess that is a human's view.
Miracles have been performed by the followers, just as Jesus did!
        People's lives have been transformed.

    I'm totally convinced now
–and I have seen it in hundreds of believers –
    that we have the Breath of God in us – the Holy Spirit!
The same as Jesus had!
    And I am sure that every believer will have the same experience –
        though I realise not all will have the wind,
        or tongues of fire
        or a dove alighting.
        Or even the speaking in languages other than our own!
            But they will have the power!

    As for me, I am convinced that God is no longer out there
somewhere, like we Jews used to believe.
He was in Christ; and now he is in each one of us.
The Holy Spirit is upon all who believe,
    and what we have seen and done
    can be repeated in different forms for all who follow Jesus.
May it be so for you!

† I have not provided references here for all the gospel passages drawn upon. Except for Luke 4, part of which is set in Nazareth, the story is about someone from that city who has come to a slowly emerging faith. The stories referred to appear in various places, though mainly Luke's gospel, and his further writings in "The Acts of the Apostles."

The Innkeeper of Jericho and other Eye-Witnesses from the Beginning

Joel of Capernaum

(Luke 4:31-41; 5:17-26)

"Your loving son, Joel."
He writes on the bottom of a scroll, then unrolls the scroll and reads from the top.
Now let me read that back.
"My dearest Father and Mother.

I hope you are both well. I am fine. I know you are wondering about me and why I left so suddenly. But I felt I had to go with Jesus. So much happened in the week I left.

You will recall the problems I was having. Indeed, how could you ever forget! The moods, the depression, the voices in my head; the screaming in the night and the swearing that came out of my mouth. Words that I assure you I did not mean. The shaking and the convulsing! You know how I felt! Well, not really, only one who has been through it, could really know. How it must have cut you up to see me like that! I was scared, confused and not…in control! It was almost a relief to discover that I had an evil spirit within me; but I had no idea who could rid me of it.

Mother, Father! You put up with a lot from me. Far more than you deserved! But you also only know half of what's gone on in my life. There was a time when I got into some pretty bad stuff. I'm sorry! I'm ashamed…now! I let you down and no doubt gave you much heartache and anxiety. I guess you just put it down to me being a teenager, and assumed all parents had to endure this sort of thing at some stage. When I think about what I was into, it shouldn't surprise me that an evil spirit came along. My lifestyle made it easy for "It!" Please don't blame yourselves. You're great parents! You deserve better!

I am not even sure how I managed to be at the synagogue the day Jesus came to Capernaum. Perhaps it was meant to be! You always encouraged us to go, but in the state I was in, I might not have been let in. As usual "It" took over. I'm disgusted now that I screamed at Jesus. That "It" through me, screamed at Jesus. However, "It" as evil as it was, knew who Jesus is. Whereas I didn't – then! "The holy one of God!" "It" shouted. "It" thought he had come to destroy it. The thought – as much as any thought was possible – crossed my mind too … briefly! And what would have happened to me if "It" was destroyed.

After the scene "It" caused in the synagogue, anything could have happened. I'm sure the Pharisees and the rabbis were not too impressed. Doesn't seem to take much to upset them! Jesus was calm, though! But firm! He simply ordered "It" out of me. "It" screamed! Shook me violently till my back teeth rattled, and left me! I fell in a heap on the ground, partly I suspect from this violent exit. And partly out of pure exhaustion! I physically felt something leave me – like invisible vomit! A feverish flush spilling out of me, like I had swallowed hot coals and belched up steam! Then I felt calmer and more relaxed than I had in ages.

The next thing I was aware of, looking up from the synagogue tiles, was the crowd gathered around Jesus. But he was looking down at me, straight into my eyes, which may have been shaken shut for a few moments. The people were looking at each other and asking who this was. And what kind of new teaching this was! I must confess, I was wondering too, even though "It" had seemed to know who he was. Whoever he was, this man had power over evil spirits. They even obeyed him! The people were saying they had never heard teaching with such authority as he had been giving in the synagogue and now demonstrated by this ... this... er...exorcism. I would have liked to have stolen a glance at the rabbis after that. I bet they were not pleased!

Jesus left with the crowd and I never got a chance to speak to him. It actually took me a while to even get up. I was just thunderstruck by what was happening and what was being said. Didn't even get a chance to say "thank you" properly! When I left, the courtyard was abuzz. Word spread quickly. Remember how, when I arrived home, our neighbour had already told you what had happened. I wasn't much help explaining things to you either. Sorry! I was still digesting it myself. I think I was in shock.

I also never told you where I went after the evening meal. I needed to talk to someone who understood me – no offence! I hadn't said too many good things to my friends for a while. I guess I needed to know if I still had any. So I went to see Bart and a few friends at his place.
Bart's the one I went to school with; then got paralysed when he fell off a roof in a work accident. Well, they had heard what had happened and whilst a little apprehensive, were glad to see me. We talked about all

sorts of things. Like I said, they hadn't been able to have a civil conversation with me for a while, so we had some catching up to do.

We kept coming back to Jesus. Other than what had happened to me that day, I had to admit I knew little. We all agreed that he had a power and authority we had never seen before. Perhaps, like the "It" had said through my lips – perhaps, he really was from God. Then I said something and I didn't know where on earth it came from. Just like the evil spirit's rantings, only this time it was for good and made sense.

"Bart," I said slowly, "I believe that if Jesus could heal me, he could make you walk again." The room was silent! Then Bart said, "Well, it's definitely worth a try. All the other physicians, healers, miracle workers, herbal cures, salt baths, prayers and massages – even laying on of hands – have done little or nothing." We laughed. "Have you tried them all?" "Yep! And look at me! I have nothing to lose. But from what Joel has said, I believe it too!"

"He has probably moved on by now!" said one of the others. But I was confident! "He's bound to come back again ... one day... I hope."

As I walked home I realised that this comment was because I so desperately wanted to see him again, not just for Bart's sake, but for mine. Walking home I met some people from down the street who had been over to a house in the main street where I saw a crowd earlier in the evening, but had avoided. They said that after what happened in the synagogue that day, people brought their sick and troubled to outside that house where Jesus was staying with one of his followers and healed them all! If only I had not avoided that crowd, we could have taken Bart that night. It was too late by the time I heard about this. But it may also have been too soon. Some processing was needed, I think!

Didn't matter, because he did come back! Not too many days later – sooner than I expected! Let me just say that in those days I had a lot of soul-searching to do. I told you earlier, I had been pretty astray with my life. Well, you knew that already, but it was even worse than you might have imagined. The evil presence was gone now, but it was as if the wrong doing wasn't. Actually, I chatted with Bart, alone on another occasion. You know how some people think his accident was punishment from God. I mean, he'd been playing up a bit too. Well, neither of us really knew whether this was how it worked – doesn't sound like a loving God – but we still felt, sorta,...empty deep inside! As if there was unfinished business! That maybe God wanted to do more in our lives. Well, he needed healing. But I needed a new direction!

Anyhow, a few days later, word gets round – pretty quickly as always – that Jesus is back in town. I rushed around to Bart's place as soon as I could, to tell him I would organise the others to take him to Jesus. If there had been more than three at his place, I would have missed them. Thom was about to come and get me to make up the foursome to carry Bart on his stretcher. Apart from the fact that Bart was no lightweight to carry in the heat of the day, we didn't know where we were going.

Then we turned a corner and saw the crowd. You would have thought tickets were on sale for the gladiator games. There were crowds of people spilling out on the street, at the house where Jesus obviously was. It was also pretty clear there were a fair few that were not locals. I could hear Judean accents, and saw Pharisees in their finery. But as we got closer, above the quietness of a spellbound crowd, I could hear Jesus' voice, even from outside.

In an unnecessary understatement, Thom expressed all our thoughts. "We'll never get him in there!" But I told you Bart had been a builder, and fell off a roof. He knew what rooves were made of, so that is where he suggested we go. "Take me up there. Make a hole and lower me down on ropes." We were flabbergasted! Thom had to run off and get some ropes. Again, I listened to Jesus' teaching. It just made so much sense to me. Anyway, to keep this letter short, when Thom returned, we did as Bart had suggested.

As we made a hole in the roof, bits of rubbish tumbled down onto the crowd below. At first, Jesus ignored us. It was as if he was waiting for the hole to be big enough to see us. He kept on teaching. Now, hearing his voice more clearly, I noted how gentle it was, yet firm and more authoritative than I had ever heard. Except perhaps at the synagogue, earlier in the week! And not like our rabbis! Speaking of which, I saw a 'gaggle' of them before we had the hole big enough for Bart. Some of them I recognised from our synagogue; but others, as I suggested before, seemed to have come a distance to get there. They were whispering intently among themselves, looking agitated, occasionally jabbing the air with their fingers and shaking their heads. They clearly weren't as impressed with Jesus' words as I was.

So we lowered Bart down. Jesus looked up before he reached the floor. But he didn't look straight at Bart. He looked past him to us. To me! Our eyes met. A smile played on his face. He clearly remembered me. He saw right through me – it was like he saw right into my soul. His eyes were filled with love and tenderness. I knew then and there that even if Bart wasn't healed, something more had happened to me that day. Then Jesus looked at Bart. But as he spoke I could still feel an eye on me.

"Your sins are forgiven you!" He said. The emptiness I spoke of before left me. And Bart too, he told me later! That's what I needed for my healing to be complete. Bart was getting it in the reverse order to me. Forgiveness first, healing second!

As you can imagine, the know-all teachers of the Law, were immediately on their high horses – sneering and saying in an audible stage whisper, "No one can forgive sins but God!" You know, they were probably right! The only thing is, they didn't realise they were in the presence of God himself or one sent from God. He challenged them in response. They might have thought he didn't hear them. It was clear that to Jesus, forgiveness and healing fitted together. Each needed to happen; doesn't matter what order they happen in.

So he said to Bart. "Get up, take your bed, and go home!" As much as I suspected it, I nearly fell through the roof with joy, when my mate got to his feet and walked again! Even though tentatively, at first, like a toddler! Jesus added, more to the crowd than to Bart and me, "This is to show you I have authority to forgive sins." Wow! Authority to cast out demons! Teaching with authority! Authority to even forgive sins! Miraculous healing power! That evil spirit of mine was right! Surely Jesus was from God! Surely he is the Messiah!

Father, Mother! I knew then that I had to go with Jesus. To follow and listen to him, and understand this power of God better! To know where that love in his eyes comes from and to know how I can best serve him! I'm coming home soon. Not because I have learnt all I can from him. I'd love to be in his presence the rest of my life – and go with him wherever he goes. I'll never tire of listening to his words and stories and watching his power at work in the lives of others. But if all that means anything, I need to serve him. The best way I can do that is not by staying with him, but by telling others of his love and power. By telling my story to those who can't go to him. It is a bit like staying in the synagogue or the Temple, waiting for people to come and hear the teaching. Many won't come. We have to go to them. He's made me aware of gifts I can share with others. So, I'll be back to do this for him. He'll no doubt be back in Capernaum again, and I'll be so pleased to see him again; eat with him even.

I have so much to tell you when I get home. I have so much to tell everyone – indeed anyone who'll listen. Even some who don't want to, will hear my story! Hearing my story, someone they know, can introduce them to God's love in a more dynamic way than those rabbis could ever do. So often their head knowledge and religious jargon and rules make it too hard for people to follow God. Jesus can't go everywhere himself; or stay where he goes for long periods. He wants people like us to help him. To be his hands and feet, his eyes and mouth! We've already seen how powerful this can be.

Shalom to you both. I look forward to seeing you soon.

Your loving son, Joel"

Grace at a Pharisee's Table

(Luke 7:36-50; John 8:1-11; Luke 8:1-3)

When I heard that he was there,
I knew,
I had to go there again.
This time,
I needed to;
last time
I needed to
because others dragged me there.
This time
only dragging would have stopped me.

The religious leaders
were doing their role,
according to them;
they brought a sinful woman
to be judged,
to a rabbi, Jesus,
whom they did not know
was the son of God,
I would discover later.
They had caught me,
at my job,
pleasuring men,
for money.

They dragged me to him;
one hand clutching my torn cloth,
the other clutching a ready stone.
When I saw him
from near the ground,
he was teaching – peacefully.
The religious leaders,
I would later discover,
were out to trap him,
test him on the Law.

"We found this woman
committing adultery."
They did not say with whom,
but let me say,
I knew every birthmark amongst them.
"We found this woman,
in the act of sinning;
and by Moses' Law
she ought to die."
Implication:
"Give us the go-ahead,
or you are complicit
in her sinning,
and also ought to die."

He knelt down;
our eyes met.
He drew in the sand
with his finger,
whilst theirs were waving
and pointing.
No, not drawing, writing!
I was the only one
of that day's crowd,
who saw what he wrote.
Lists of sins;
not mine.
Their fingers and their voices
kept jabbing at the air
around me, around us.
Straightening up,
he agreed.
But,
"Let he who is without sin
cast the first stone."
He had done it.
He had sentenced me, I thought,

not grasping the weight of his words.

I cowered.
I waited
for that first stone to strike me,
Instead, I heard
"a plop!"
And another!
And another!
I dared to look around me.
I saw them turning away from me, from us.
The stones "plopping" on the ground
next to me.
The "plops" continued.
It seemed like the falling
of my sins
onto the ground around me.

Then, but for the outer ring
who had watched this with me,
only he and I remained.
"Where are they?"
He asked, as if to stress a point.
"Who condemns you?"
"No one .... Sir!"
I couldn't believe it;
nor what followed.
"Then neither do I!
Go your way!
Your sins are forgiven!"

A weight had been taken from me.
My sins had "plopped"
next to a dozen or more stones.
My real desire
was to stay;
to hear

what he was teaching
the crowds that surrounded us.
Perhaps what motivated him
to say what he had said to me:
"Your sins are forgiven!"
But he said, "Go!"
So I did.
The gravity of this all,
hadn't quite sunk in:
inside a part of me
challenged whether staying was safe;
another part desired
to stay and savour
this forgiveness
for all it was worth,
like rocks of gold,
not the rocks of death
that lay around me.

And so, when I heard
he was at a meal
in Simon the Pharisee's house
(a house I knew well),
I knew I had to go.
Ironic,
for if Simon wasn't there with a stone
when I first met Jesus,
his companions that night, were.
Enough to deter me, perhaps;
but, no, nothing could drag me
away.
I needed to see Jesus
again.
To see his eyes;
to hear his voice;
to thank him
for freeing me;

if any of this was possible.
And if Simon
had his way with me
(in a different way to last time I saw him);
I would still die a happy woman
forgiven,
free,
happy, again.

We all
at some time,
do something
on impulse;
that we can't explain.
Going to Simon's house that night,
was not one of these;
but taking an alabaster jar
of ointment,
stock of my previous trade,
was!

In our culture,
meals with community guests
were community events;
and so,
the doors of Simon's house
were open to all and sundry.
Not that sundry
reclined at the master's table
(especially not the women),
but that they could hear
the accompanying words
and learn from them.
No doubt,
when I appeared,
Simon sneered
and would have liked

to have me barred,
thrown onto the street again.
But he wasn't about to make a scene,
yet!
From a narrowing distance,
as I approached,
I saw Jesus welcomed
to the table;
but his feet were not washed,
his head was not anointed,
his cheeks were not kissed.
His host was not hospitable,
belying his true intentions;
his true feelings for Jesus.

As I have said,
we all at some time,
do something by impulse.
Seeing this rejection,
my heart sank for him;
but the jar pressed against my hip.
He had forgiven me;
for that I loved him,
and welcome him I must.
I took a position at his feet,
as he reclined at the table.
A gasp was palpable
in the room;
within my chest,
my heartbeat too, was palpable.
I wept.
I was so sad for him.
These were tears of sadness,
and of gratitude;
gratitude for an act that deserved
better treatment, better welcome,
than Simon was giving him.

I washed his feet
with those tears;
I dried those tears,
with my hair,
shamelessly let loose.
I kissed his feet
with my lips
that wanted to cry out.
I anointed him
with that ointment.
So grateful was I!

Simon muttered,
to himself, he thought.
Clearly Jesus heard,
and so did I;
or else some instinct
cried out, within us.
He questioned whether this could be a prophet,
if he allowed such a sinful woman,
to let down her hair,
to touch him,
to kiss him
in such a provocative way.
"Simon," he replied.
"Yes, Teacher,"
like a cat caught in the act,
cream dripping from his lips.
I waited for Jesus to scold him;
well I hoped Jesus would scold him,
as he did amidst the hand-held stones
in the market-place.
He didn't.
He told a story.
He told a story
of a creditor
with two debtors;

one owed fifty
another five hundred.
Neither could repay.
So the creditor
cancelled the debts;
both of them.
Another palpable gasp!
"Which one will love him more?"
Quite simple!
Even I, a woman, could answer that one.
And so could Simon.

Then Jesus looked at me.
Our eyes met;
as they had midst that pile of stones.
I felt accepted, unjudged and unafraid;
just as in the marketplace.
But he spoke to Simon, his host.
"Do you see this woman?"
Course he did; how could he not?
No, of course he had not!
For to do so, was beneath him.
"When I entered your house:
you gave me no water for my feet;
no towel to dry them;
no oil to anoint my head;
no kiss of welcome for my cheeks.
When she entered your house,
unwelcomed:
she washed my feet with her tears;
she dried them with her hair;
she has smothered them with kisses;
she anointed them with ointment.
Her sins which were many,
are forgiven."
For a moment he stole a glance at his host,
saying,

"But the one to whom little is forgiven,
loves little."
He looked at me again.
My eyes were ready this time.
His face glistened in my tears.
"Your sins are forgiven."
His words were more golden
than those on the roadside.
"Your faith has saved you.
Go in peace!"
It was a lot like that first time.
You want to stay.
But you are told to go.
I did.
But I was back.
I followed him forever after;
along with other women
who had received the same gift as me;
not knowing that I had that night;
anointed him for his death.
The death that such acts
of forgiveness
are want to lead to ,
because of the hatred of people
like Simon.
But that hatred will never win;
and it didn't this time.

---

† This is the poem, to which I refer in the 'Introduction', that is my only attempt to write in a woman's voice. It is also one of my more recent pieces, so perhaps it is the product of my maturing as a storywriter. Note it brings together two stories from different gospels, so this is part of the creative edge. It just seemed to me that these two stories, unique to different gospels, might fit together; but for whatever reason, and a number could be suggested, neither of these gospel compilers thought so.

The Innkeeper of Jericho and other Eye-Witnesses from the Beginning

"How Strong is your faith?"

(Matthew 9:9-13; 18-26)

How strong is your faith?
Sorry to be so personal;
    you probably don't expect to be asked such a personal question.
(Especially, if you have heard it when you have come to church!)
But, hey, it is all right! I'm happy to share a secret or two of my own.

    Can you imagine how I felt when Jesus walked right up to me
        at the tax booth, where I collected taxes,
            and said, "Matthew, follow me!"
The thing is that it was an answer to prayer.

    I was going nowhere!
Because of my job, I was an outcast and hated by my people.
The Romans forced tax collectors to deceive
    and steal from our own people.
I had just hoped there was some way to regain some self-esteem.
To turn my back on this job
    and be accepted again as a valued member of the community!
Big ask! As a tax collector for the Roman Empire,
    there was no such hope – even if I had resigned.
No one was about to come and free me from all this.
Well, that is what I had thought! But God answered my prayer.
My faith was rewarded – but at the same time tested – big-time!
    It is relatively easy to pray a prayer
        you don't really expect to be answered.

    Maybe you have done that sometimes.
Well, whatever I expected deep down;
    God answered my prayer, through Jesus.
But it tested my faith more than praying the prayer in the first place.
Jesus said to me, "Follow me!"
Instantly, somehow, I knew what he meant!
Namely: "Get up! Leave your job! Leave all those tax monies!
    Do not hesitate!

Do not sharpen your pencil! Leave everything and follow me!
Do not even ask where we are going or what it will cost!"
What about it? I ask you.
Could you respond positively to a call like that?
"Yes, Lord, whatever you say!"
Or more likely: "Hang on, I have things to tidy up here!"
"I have a life to sort out first!"
"I couldn't leave the security of my lifestyle."

If any of these thoughts went through my mind,
they did so pretty quickly.
And I don't think it is because there is nothing there to slow it down;
despite what some people might think!
No, it was that Jesus should even bother to speak to me,
let alone call me to follow him.
I knew this rabbi – had seen him around –
but I guess I never really thought
that he would be interested in a rogue and an outcast like me.
The fact that he did, was enough for me.
My faith within me welled up;
and it seemed like nothing to just get up and go.
To follow him, as he requested!

He explained this acceptance of me later at the meal table,
when I invited him over to my house,
where I had gathered some friends and fellow tax collectors.
Open house; open table; as it is in our culture!
So, not totally surprisingly, some Pharisees appeared!
They must have heard that he
(a religious person wanting to be taken seriously)
had dared to speak to me
(a sinner and an outcast and a traitor to the Jews).
So naturally they complained to him that he even bothered
to mix with sinners like me.
He answered them:
"Those who are well" – meaning them – "don't need a doctor.
It's the sick" – like me – "that needs one!"

He said he came desiring mercy,
        rather than the sort of sacrifices
                those self-centered teachers were proud of themselves
                      for making.
"I have come to call, not the righteous, but sinners to repentance."
It made me wonder. Who are the real sick people – them or us?
Who needs him most?

        But I digress. I was talking about faith.
You might think I showed a fair bit of faith by rising and following him.
But let me tell you what happened later
      and see where you would draw the line.
How strong is your faith?

        Not long after all this,
                a leader of the synagogue came to Jesus in the street.
I was soon to discover that there were people coming all the time.
The sick, the outcast; but also influential people like this one!
Most came seeking healing;
      or maybe forgiveness; often in a roundabout sort of way.
Or to test him!
A lot of teachers of the Law and religious leaders
      were really only doing that.

        But this leader from the synagogue was different.
With humility and grace, but with steely determination,
      he knelt at Jesus' feet and said
            – in an almost "matter of fact" sort of way:
                "My daughter has just died;
                but come, lay your hand on her,
                and she shall live."
Whoa there! That is one big ask!
I was the new one in the pack;
      so I expected one of Jesus' other followers
      to quietly send him away with a
            "That's a bit much to ask of him!"
But if anyone was going to do that, Jesus made the first move.

He beckoned the leader up, and followed him – immediately!
I thought afterwards, he followed almost as quickly as I did.

    Now it was clear that this leader of the synagogue had great faith.
There was not one hint of hesitation in his voice. No uncertainty at all!
He fully believed that Jesus could raise his daughter from the dead.
And Jesus was prepared to respond to his request –
    he went without hesitating, and followed this faithful father.

    I might add,
    he did so once again to reach out to one of the least important.
First me – an unclean sinner and outcast;
    now an insignificant child – and a girl at that!
You need to understand that in my culture, women, children, the sick
    and the unclean, just do not rate.
But this man of God was prepared to reach out to even these.
    Even to the dead!
    Have I lost you yet?
Could you contemplate for one minute that Jesus could or would raise
    a person from the dead – whoever that person might be.
I have to admit that I was struggling.

    As I have heard about the world from afar in the centuries
        that have passed since,
        I know others have raised people from the dead
            – in God's name.
The only reason such things don't happen more often
    is surely for lack of faith.
Although sometimes God has other plans,
    and a release from earthly life
        is the right 'healing' for some people.
But this was a child! Still rocks you, doesn't it? Does it?
Could you have the faith that leader had – even for your own child?
    But there's more! Much more!

    As we followed the leader of the synagogue
through the milling crowd, a woman came up.

> Actually, she crept up.

None of us saw her coming amidst the crowd.
Apparently she had been bleeding for twelve years!
Permanently unclean and therefore outcast for twelve years!
There's that 'O' word again! Can you contemplate that?
And a woman as well,
> so that got her off to a bad start before she even got sick.

Our cultural thing again!
> You might think of who we are talking about in your community
> > or wider society.

Anyway, she must have been so desperate.

> Desperation calls for desperate acts –

or maybe gives great faith and hope.
Maybe such a person would hope for anything,
> having been let down so many times.
> > By society!
> > By medical people!
> > Maybe even by friends, neighbours and family!
> But her faith was great!

You see, we discovered that she believed that just touching Jesus' cloak would heal her.
> This would be enough!

Most people would expect something that could be seen.
A touch from the master!
Some special words or a prayer invoking God to heal her!
No, she believed an anonymous touch would be sufficient!
But there is another reason for anonymity!
Not only was she determined, and desperate, and full of faith;
> this was a courageous and dangerous thing to do.

As a bleeding woman, she was unclean!
She had no right to be in that crowd; out in the public!
Our Law views that with the strongest condemnation.
Furthermore, to touch Jesus would have made him unclean also.
Yet, because of her faith and his healing power,
> that touch made them both clean again!

Again, he did not reject her or turn her away for who she was.

"Take heart!" He said. "Your faith has made you well."
  And it was so!

If you can even contemplate the gravity of her situation,
is your faith great enough to believe this could happen to you?
To anyone you know? Only you can answer that! Ultimately you must!
  Or maybe you couldn't!
Would you have put yourself in that situation to know?

  And the dead girl? Raised as instantly as the woman was healed!
If I saw nothing more, that day convinced me of the great power –
  of God unleashed!
On the one hand, by the faith of ordinary people, like you and I;
  and on the other hand, by Jesus' rejection of the norms
    of our society and the Law.
I wonder where you are, in this.
Metaphorically or literally:
  in the bind I was living in;
  desperately seeking release like that woman
    (albeit of quite a different situation).
  Or maybe expectant because of some person or thing
    you have lost, like the father.
  And in a way that was me also.

  You write your own script!
Then have you the faith to let God finish it?
Hear him say, "Follow me!"
 Hear him say, "Take heart, your faith has made you well!"
Get up then!
And when you do, and have seen God's power at work in your life,
  then go spread the word throughout the community.
Do what you can to spread the stories of our faith.
Like those you have heard today.
 Then others may be made well,
  and experience God's love and grace too.

  Shalom!

An Israeli Shepherd speaks

You city people don't understand us shepherds, do you?
Yes, I'm a shepherd. From Israel – of the old school, if you like!
Our methods haven't changed much in thousands of years,
    until fairly recently.

To know how we operate,
 you've got to understand the relationship we have with our sheep.
You also may not realise their importance in our culture and our religion.

For example, our sheep are like children to us.
We know them, each individually. Know them by name!
    They know our voices. So they come to us. They follow us.
Course, our flocks have been relatively small, so we can lead them.
Not like in some countries today, where the flocks are large
    and are driven with people and dogs even, I hear, behind them.
We lead them – to pastures, to water, to shelter, and home again at night.
We provide their needs, protect them, sleep with them to keep them safe.

No wonder, when Jesus spoke of being a good shepherd,
    it led to him talking of love and of him laying down
        his life for his sheep.
I don't know that I could go that far.
But of course, that was a metaphor for him.
His flock was a human one, and much greater than mine.

    Shepherds are at the forefront of Jewish history,
culture and religion.
Indeed these three important pillars that inform our identity
    are very much intertwined.
    We are a rural people and our livelihood has always been closely
    linked with the land and its produce –
        especially raising flocks and herds
            -but also growing crops and fruit.
So imagery from this country life has helped us understand
    who we are and what we believe.

And has played an important part in our long history!

    Adam's son, Abel, raised sheep,
and his sacrifice pleased Yahweh.
    Cain's, of grain, did not. Cain was jealous and killed his brother.

    The Patriarchs had flocks – Abraham and his family;
Jacob and his family, including Joseph. Then Moses!

    In the Law, the requirement was given that a sheep be sacrificed
        for the atonement of sins.
At the first Passover,
    the night our people were led from slavery in Egypt, by Moses,
    the best sheep had to be sacrificed,
    and its blood smeared on the doorposts.
Where there was no blood,
    which was all Egyptian homes
        because they didn't know what Yahweh had ordered;
            the oldest of the household died.
All the meat had to be eaten, before they set off for freedom.
We still remember that night at the Feast of the Passover.
The story is retold each year.
It was at such a re-telling and re-enacting,
    that Jesus celebrated with his disciples, the night before he died.

    But I move too fast!
In the Promised Land the people raised flocks.
Our greatest king, David, was a shepherd boy.
He wrote about sheep and shepherds in some of his Psalms.
The most famous one of which has become known as number 23.
But there are other references to sheep and shepherds.
Also the people of Israel are likened to sheep;
    the Lord being their shepherd.
Jesus calls himself the "good shepherd", as I have already mentioned.
Yahweh promised Abraham,
    his people would be Yahweh's chosen people.
And he entered into covenants with them that spoke of this relationship.

So the Psalm speaks of Yahweh feeding and protecting his flock,
    like a shepherd would.

    When David sinned his great sin –
committing adultery with Bathsheba
and having Uriah, her husband, killed,
        the prophet, Nathan, used a story about the sheep of a poor man,
            being stolen by a rich sheep owner.
It showed David, his sin. And he was cut deeply by the story!
 Remember he had been a shepherd!

    Some of the prophets were shepherds!
They also spoke not only of Yahweh as a shepherd,
      but also of the coming Messiah, as being like one.
The imagery of sheep was used to understand not only our relationship
      with Yahweh, but also our behaviours.
 For example, "all we like sheep have gone astray."
I can tell you, there's never been a truer word spoken.
    I can vouch for "straying."
In the case of the people of Israel, one result of this was the exile.
 The people had "their" Promised Land, taken from them.
 Later it was returned to a remnant.

    Somewhere, this rosy view of shepherds,
        and heroes of our faith who had tended sheep, fell apart.
The teachers of the Law in Jesus' day, considered shepherds "unclean"!
    A so-called "proscribed profession"!
You see, increasingly it became necessary
    to take our sheep further afield, to find pastures for them.
We were accused of dishonesty
    and theft because our sheep grazed onto other people's land.
We were cast to the edges of society,
    being "unclean"; like tax collectors and prostitutes.
You don't know how much that hurts.
Especially when they still needed our sheep for their sacrifices
    in the Temple!

I think Yahweh had the last laugh! I think he loves us shepherds!
I mean, take for example, the birth of Jesus, his son.
The news was first revealed to – a bunch of ordinary shepherds!
Imagine what those religious leaders and teachers of the Law
    would have thought if they knew that unclean shepherds
        were chosen to be the earliest witnesses
            to the birth of the Messiah.
Of course they didn't hear the story at the time!
    And they didn't believe he was the Messiah!
        We didn't at first, either!
But when you hear how Jesus saw himself
    as a shepherd of his people,
        it sort of helps guys like me to understand and believe.

    Our culture remained a rural one, and Jesus understood this.
When he taught, he used stories with lots of images
    of produce of the land – sheep and grain and seeds and vines.
For example, he told a parable about a shepherd
    who lost one sheep from a flock of a hundred;
        and he left the others to go search for it.
He rejoiced when he returned home with it.
That rejoicing, Jesus said,
    was like what happens in heaven when a lost person is saved.
You get that?
    Jesus is saying that Yahweh is like a shepherd
        – an unclean shepherd!
In case, you don't know,
    Jesus told that story to Pharisees and teachers of the Law,
        who were criticising Jesus for the poor company he kept.
Stories like this tell us that Jesus understood, not only sheep,
    but people too!
He gives us an image of Yahweh's great love for all his flock –
    including us.

    When Jesus spoke of being the Good Shepherd;
he said he was even willing to lay down his life for his sheep.
Interesting that the Good Shepherd, is also the Lamb of Yahweh;

who pays the ultimate sacrifice,
  when he lays down his life on the cross.
This was the supreme sacrifice to atone for our sins for all times.
In the Temple the sacrifices had to be made on a regular basis.
Jesus ended the need for this.
 When Jesus died on the cross,
  the curtain of the Holy of Holies was ripped down.
 Not that anyone realised the significance of this at the time!

The relationship that comes from this then,
  is the one between sheep and shepherd, that I spoke of earlier.
Jeremiah spoke of a new covenant allowing us to know Yahweh
 and talk to him personally, not just through some priest in the Temple.
The relationship was demonstrated by Jesus,
  the Good Shepherd, and what he did for his sheep.
It is summed up by one word – LOVE!
Jesus spoke of loving one another as he has loved us.
His love was so great that he would, as I said,
  lay down his life for his friends.
We may never do that; but we must love one another.
It is this love that identifies us as part of his new flock –
  Followers! Believers!
And the only way to show this love is to put it into action.
He did! His love was not just words – but actions!
We too are called to act out of our love.

  Anyway, I better go. My sheep are calling me!

---

† I have not attempted to list the references used here, stretching as they do across both Jewish and Christian Scriptures.

The Road to Jerusalem

(Luke 8:1-3; 19: 28-48; 22:1 – 24:49)

My name is Cleopas.
You may know of me from the story best-known as
    "The Road to Emmaus".
I want to tell you the story of the other road we travelled often.
    The road to Jerusalem!
By "we" I mean my companion and me.
This companion was not named there, in that story;
    so I shall not be the one to reveal an identity here.

Of course we travelled the road to Emmaus often too.
Emmaus is a small town some seven miles or eleven kilometres
    roughly west of Jerusalem.
Of insignificant size, it may be 'lost' by scholars in future millennia.[10]
But we knew where it was!
Our story has put it 'on the map' and in the scriptures, for all time.

We had travelled the road to Jerusalem
    the week before the Passover.
We had family and friends there with whom we were to share this feast
    of Unleavened Bread.
We were among crowds of extra pilgrims who would be coming
    to the city for the Festival.
But we had heard that Jesus of Nazareth would be coming to the city,
    and we had hoped to see him.

We knew Jesus to be a "prophet mighty in word and deed
    before God and all the people."

---

[10] "Emmaus – A Judean town now of uncertain identification, which was the destination of two travellers to whom Jesus appeared after his crucifixion. ... For the identification of this town, the only clue given by Luke is that it was 7 ½ miles from Jerusalem. All external evidence and all traditions direct the attention westward from Jerusalem; nevertheless there are no fewer than four modern towns proposed as NT Emmaus, ranging from 4 miles to 20 miles from Jerusalem."

The Interpreters' Dictionary of the Bible Vol. 2, Abingdon Press, Nashville, 1984 (14th Printing. First Published 1962) p. 97-98

Furthermore, "we had hoped he was the one to redeem Israel"
>from the Romans.
We thought maybe, that this was his time;
>when this redemption might be achieved.
So here was another reason to come to Jerusalem.
>Jesus was travelling down from Galilee,
>>where most of his teaching and "mighty" acts had taken place.
We had met him there on a trip we made up north a year or so ago.
Now, he would come to Jerusalem through Jericho,
>travelling in from the north east.
(I mention this to distinguish his entry point into Jerusalem from ours.)

>As we came to the outskirts of Jerusalem,
we saw the crowds of people heading into the city that we had expected.
Our road to Jerusalem joined another,
>more major one that came from Joppa,
>>on the coast of the Mediterranean Sea.
As we came closer we saw that it wasn't just crowds of pilgrims;
>it was a procession.

>It was quickly clear what this procession was,
but we still asked.[11]
>"What's going on?"
Some of the crowd reminded us that the Roman governor, Pontus Pilate,
>came in from his coastal home for the Passover.
"Why? He is no Jew, to celebrate our Festival!"
"No!" came the reply. "You are right.
>But he likes to remind us who is in charge,
>>by bringing a show of force to the city of Jerusalem
>>when so many Jews are there,
>>>not just from Jerusalem
>>>>but from outlying areas of Judea.
Apparently Herod is here from Galilee also.

---

[11] The idea of a second procession on the day the Church celebrates as 'Palm Sunday' was explored in:
Marcus Borg and John Dominic Crossan, *The Last Week: A day by day account of Jesus' final week in Jerusalem,* Harper One, San Francisco, 2006

For a similar reason, no doubt,
> though he wastes no love on the Romans – and Pilate."

"A show of force, indeed!"
I observed, as column after column of Roman soldiers,
> all decked out in glistening battle armour,
>> proceeded on fine horses.

There was the centurion, dressed in his finery,
> and seated on a fine white steed.

Then of course, Pilate himself, just as resplendent, but not in battle attire
> – riding in a fancy carriage,
>> flanked by the protection of more mounted soldiers,
>>> with their weapons on full show,
>>>> as though they were marching into battle.

They weren't, of course; but nor were they arriving to the welcome
> accorded a victorious army, or the heroes of the homeland.

The odd game local booed and hissed; but fairly quietly,
> for it was clear that secret police scurried furtively
> throughout the crowd, watching for any opposition,
> and seizing on any such comments of dissent.

So these were kept amongst friends; but we still heard plenty of them!

> Had we lived in Bethphage or Bethany
and been entering Jerusalem at a similar time
> from that Jericho side of town,
>> we would have seen a different procession.

Before the Sabbath which followed that Passover
> and "the things that happened there in those days,"
>> we heard only snippets about that procession.

On the Sabbath the full story emerged. But I get ahead of myself!

> Jesus of Nazareth entered the city seated on a mere colt –
> a donkey.

He was surrounded by his disciples, many other followers
> and the women that had followed him from Galilee.

Some waved palm branches; some had thrown their cloaks on the road.
Crowds of his followers "praised God joyfully with loud shouts,
> for the deeds of power that they had seen",

of which we were also aware.

"Blessed is the king who comes in the name of the Lord!
Peace in heaven and glory in the highest heaven!"

This was the high praise that the subject of the other procession,
the one we saw on our side of the city, would have appreciated.
Unlike at that procession,
here some opponents of Jesus knew they could speak up.
Some Pharisees were heard to tell Jesus,
"Order your disciples to be quiet!"
But he answered,
"I tell you if these were silent, the stones would start shouting."

Later, once we had been to our accommodation,
we went to worship at the Temple,
having not been there since our last visit.
Officers of the Temple guard blocked our path.
There had been 'an incident' and the Temple courtyard was closed.
We peered between these soldiers and thought we caught
a glimpse of chaos within the courtyard market.

Like every Jew, we knew about the market.
The requirement that only the best birds and sheep could be sacrificed,
and to safeguard this purity, they needed to be purchased there.
Then there was the decree that visitors from outside of town
had to make their monetary offering using the Temple currency,
to which was attached an exchange rate.
Both transactions attracted lofty fees which the chief priests imposed
in order to boost the coffers of the Temple.
It made access to the Temple something that could be accomplished
by only those with the wealth to do so.
We always thought this smacked of values not consistent
with what Temple worship represented.

So what had happened before our arrival?
People who had been required to leave after this 'incident'

were very willing to tell us.
A rabbi had entered the Temple grounds, and seemed disturbed,
    by what, as I have said, we are used to
        – the market, corrupt as it was known to be.
Not surprisingly, he took exception to what he saw.
He drove out the money changers,
    overturning their tables,
        splashing coins across the tiled stone floors.
He freed the birds from their cages; the sheep from their pens.
He took a bound rope, and wielding it like a whip,
    he cried with a loud voice:
        "My house shall be a house of prayer;
        but you have made it a den of robbers."
That was why he was disturbed.
Immediately, we knew it was Jesus of Nazareth.
Immediately, we seized upon "my house,"
    and knew more about this
        "prophet mighty before God and all the people."

We made another attempt to visit the Temple next day,
    when all was more or less back to normal!
But we were astounded to see Jesus teaching there.
After what had happened the day before,
    we imagined the chief priests and Temple guards
    would have stopped him doing this.
But the people seemed spellbound by what he taught,
    and by weight of numbers,
        the leaders seemed afraid to act against him.
It didn't stop them offering their comments from the back rows!
We heard later Jesus went daily to teach in the Temple that week;
    and had we known,
        we would have gone back because we loved what he said
        when we were there.

Behind the scenes, we later discovered that Judas Iscariot,
one of the twelve, made a deal with the religious leaders,
    to betray Jesus to them, when the crowds were not around,

in exchange for money.
Well, it all unravelled after that.
Jesus ate the Passover with the twelve.
They would later tell us about his arrest in the Mount of Olives garden,
    after he had prayed there.
They sheepishly acknowledged they ran away when this happened.
Next day we saw the crowds in the Jerusalem street
    outside Pilate's residence, baying for him to be crucified.
We wondered whether some of these people
    had been present cheering him
    as he entered the city at the beginning of the week.
Or maybe they were curious onlookers then,
    who had now had their minds made up for them
        about who Jesus was.
Pilate finally gave in to the religious leaders' urges.
He had seemed reluctant for some time, seeking to release Jesus.
Then we followed another ugly procession up Skull hill,
    also called Golgotha.
There he was nailed to a cross, along with a couple of villains.

    We had never been to a crucifixion; not in a hurry to go again.
It is a torturous way to die.
Apparently men can hang on a cross for many hours,
    even into the next day.
But this was the day before the Sabbath, and it was important to Judaism
    that those crucified be down off the cross
        and taken away before sunset on the Friday.
For this reason the other two men's legs were broken, to hasten their end.
    This makes breathing more difficult for one on a cross.
Jesus, died more quickly, without needing this treatment.
    He seemed to give up, willingly to death;
        committing his spirit to "his Father".
We lingered with those who knew him – men and women
    – until his body was taken away,
        and buried in a fresh tomb not far away.
And we went home, shattered, for as I said before,
    "we had hoped he was the one to redeem Israel!"

Because of the Sabbath,
    we needed to wait until the first day of the week to go home.
On the Sabbath, we spent time with some of the disciples.
They filled in many of the gaps of our knowledge of what happened.
    What he said and did at the Passover meal.
    How he talked of the coming of the Kingdom of God.
    And graphically, how he had broken bread and given it to them;
        and shared a cup of wine amongst them.
        His body broken; his blood shed –
            "For them!" He said.
Then he made reference to his death again,
    but they didn't comprehend that this was imminent.
        "Again!" because in hindsight
    we recalled that even in Galilee he had prophesied his death.
We also had forgotten or not understood
    what he said would follow this death.
At the Passover meal,
    he even indicated that his betrayer was at the table with them.
Eleven of them were shocked at this;
    but they didn't know who the other one was.

    They recounted too,
what had happened in the garden at the Mount of Olives, after the meal.
They ashamedly told of sleeping instead of praying;
    to then be admonished by Jesus for doing so.
One thought he caught bits of Jesus' prayer.
On reflection, he realised it seemed to speak
    of what was about to happen;
        and a request from Jesus that there might be another way.
Then Judas turned up with a crowd
    – chief priests, Temple guards, scribes!
        He was the betrayer!
All but Peter scuttled away in the other direction,
    deserting Jesus as he was arrested and taken away.
Peter, with a broken heart,
    told how he denied three times that he knew Jesus,

when challenged in the courtyard of the chief priest,
         fearing he may be arrested also.
At the meal, he had said to Jesus that he would go with him
       to prison and to death.
What happened between then and the trial we saw before Pilate,
       would later become someone else's story.
It was a long and difficult Sabbath day!

       The events of next day, as I have said,
 have become a well-known story now.
My friend and I returned home; trying, as we did,
       to analyse these events.
A fellow traveller joined us, who seemed to know nothing of them.
       We were astounded and sorry that there was anyone in Jerusalem
              who knew nothing of that execution.
And so we told him!
       How this death had dashed our hopes
              that this Jesus would be our redeemer,
                     as well as "a prophet, mighty in word and deed,
                            before God and all the people."
He listened quietly and respectfully to our story,
       seeming to empathise with our grief.
But then he called us
       "foolish and slow to believe that the Messiah had to suffer."
We didn't believe it; because we didn't understand it!
Over the next however many miles we travelled,
       he gave us a study of our Scriptures
       that no rabbi had ever given us before.
He talked about every verse that spoke of the prophesies
       of what the Messiah would do, and have happen to him.
Some we remembered well; others were faint memories;
       and more we hardly knew.

       By the time we got to Emmaus,
 our heads were spinning, full of scriptures.
Our companion on the road seemed to us to be some sort of rabbi
       with an impeccable knowledge of these.

We wanted to hear more.
    But it is also in the nature of our hospitable ways
        to invite such an acquaintance to come into our house;
           especially since he seemed to be going further,
              and night was fast approaching.
At the table, our guest did a most unusual thing – for a guest that is!
He took the role of the host!
He took the bread, gave thanks for it, broke it, and gave it to us.
And instantly, the two of us graphically saw the picture
    the disciples had painted of what he did at the Passover meal.
    "This is my body, broken for you!"
Immediately, we recognised him;
    though we had just spent several hours with him,
        in daylight, not recognising him.
It had been as though our eyes had been kept from doing so,
    by something we couldn't explain.
        Our companion was Jesus – alive again!
As he lifted his hands holding the bread,
    I thought I glimpsed two fresh wounds.
But it was the breaking of the bread that clinched it for us.
His action at the Passover table had been described to us so vividly.
Then, our elation was dashed, for as we recognised him,
    he vanished from our sight.

We both spoke at once – like excited schoolchildren.
    "Did not our hearts burn within us on the road?
    As he opened the Scriptures to us?"
We have seen Jesus, the Messiah, raised from the dead,
    and as he put it "entered into his glory.""
There was no question about what we needed to do next.
We had to go and tell the eleven and the other followers,
    in case they did not know.

And so we were soon on that familiar road to Jerusalem
once again, though the night had begun,
and the road was lit only by a gleeful moon, and the lantern we carried.
Were we to pass anyone else foolish enough to be out at that time,

       they would have seen our beaming faces, even in the dark.
In a different way, this walk was as important
       as the one we had made with Jesus that day.
For now we processed for ourselves, what had been mere words then.
Words that took on new significance
       because we now knew who had said them!
We went over it all again,
       taking turns to recall what we had gleaned from those words.
The scriptures about the Messiah, yes!
But noting the hints that he would indeed be victorious in his quest!
       His sojourn on earth!
Then there were the words that Jesus himself spoke,
       on numerous occasions, as his followers recalled.
That he would suffer; be handed over to sinners and be crucified!
If they didn't understand that (or was it just too hard to believe),
       they certainly didn't grasp his suggestion
              that he would rise again to life on the third day.
We had told him on the road that the women
       had been to the empty tomb,
              and saw, not a body,
                      but "a vision of angels that said he was alive."
What would women know, we thought,
       and dismissed it as a grief-filled apparition, or "an idle tale."
We still had not grasped the possibility when some of the men,
       including Peter, went and found it as the women had said.
Maybe, if we had stayed in Jerusalem on the first day,
       we may have analysed, as we had done on the Sabbath,
              and some of the gaps in our understanding
                      might have been filled.
Then we would have seen, what Jesus had told us:
       "It was necessary that the Messiah suffer these things
              (which we had experienced and spoken of on the road)
              and then enter into his glory."
And "Alleluia", some of that glory would be shared with us.

       Given we were completing something akin to the length
           of what the Greeks call 'a marathon',

                        you might expect we would have been slowing down.
I think we walked that road to Jerusalem the fastest we ever had,
            in our ecstasy.
It had not really occurred to us that maybe the disciples and the others,
        could have retired by the time we walked towards the one light
                still on in the city of Jerusalem
                        late that first night of the week.
                            Nay! early next morning.
Afterall, we thought we were the only ones who had seen the risen Jesus.
A light was certainly on!

        So we called out when we arrived,
    because a knock would have scared them,
            thinking the Romans or the Temple guards had come for them.
We were hardly in the room, with the door re-locked behind us,
        and still adjusting to who was there,
                and certainly had not had a chance to tell them our story,
                    when they burst out with:
        "The Lord has risen indeed and has appeared to Peter!"
Although she wasn't there,
        there was comment that Mary had seen him also.
I doubt they would have expected we could beat that story.
But as we recalled what had happened on the road that day,
        and that evening,
                and how we recognised him only in the breaking
                        of the bread, their mouths hung open.
If we thought we had won the day with our story,
        the surprises kept coming.

        Suddenly, though the door was locked,
Jesus stood in our midst, greeting us with "Peace be with you!"
And it was!
It most certainly was, just as it had been missing for several days.
He showed us his wounds.
Maybe he should have done that earlier on the road.
(But imagine the story that would have been lost
        if we had recognised him immediately on the road!)

He ate some fish.
The thought about when that night
    would end had not even entered my head.
But it wasn't any time soon,
    for he gave the rest the same study of the scriptures
        we had on the road to Emmaus!
How "everything written about *me* (he said this time)
    in the law of Moses,
        the prophets and the psalms had to be fulfilled."

He told us that we were witnesses of all
    that the Messiah had endured according to the Scriptures.
Henceforth, repentance and forgiveness of sins
    would be available to all people,
        and was to be proclaimed in the Messiah's name
            to all nations.
But first, we would be empowered for this work,
    with a power that came from God.

This empowerment was to happen in Jerusalem.
And from Jerusalem that proclamation was to begin!
My companion and I hurried home to Emmaus
    to tidy up our affairs there.
Then we were back on the road to Jerusalem
    for the last time, for a long time;
        very excited about what the future held,
            as we were a part of this empowering and proclamation.
And we were called to be witnesses from the beginning.

Bibliography

Aurelio, John, *Myth Man: A Storyteller's Jesus,* Crossroad Pub. Co., New York, 1992

Bailey, Kenneth E., *Jesus through Middle Eastern Eyes: Cultural Studies in the Gospels"*, IVP Academic, Illinois, 2008

Borg, Marcus & Crossan, John Dominic, *The Last Week: A day by day account of Jesus' final week in Jerusalem,* Harper One, San Francisco, 2006

Jackman, Stuart, *The Davidson Affair,* Faber and Faber, London, 1966.

Jensen, Richard A., *Thinking in Story: Preaching in a Post-Literate Age,* C.S.S. Publishing Co., Lima, Ohio, 1993

The Interpreter's Dictionary of the Bible, Abingdon Press, Nashville, 1984 (14th Printing. First Published 1962)

www.ingramcontent.com/pod-product-compliance
Lightning Source LLC
Chambersburg PA
CBHW070308010526
44107CB00056B/2524